THEN AND NOW

My Road to Survival

To ALICIA   HOPE yOU EnJOy
The RcAP

KENNETH TAYLOR

Then and Now
Copyright © 2022 by Kenneth Taylor

Tellwell Talent
www.tellwell.ca

ISBN
978-0-22888-246-6 (Hardcover)
978-0-22888-245-9 (Paperback)
978-0-22888-247-3 (eBook)

I've experienced many life journeys with a childhood of violence and abuse. Going from a home of outlaw bikers to my grandparent's house of religious beliefs. These are the stories of the bad, the good, and the funny. That makes up a great read; this book will keep you guessing from one page to the other as to what will happen next. I wrote this book to show that just because someone betrayed you and your trust. Abusing you physically and killing your trust. In someone who is supposed to love you. It doesn't mean you have to let it control your life. I know it's hard, believe me, but remember you're the one in charge. You can live the best life possible; all you have to do is want it. It can be done; never let the abuser win. This is your life, not theirs; they threw there's away. The moment they abused you. You should have many journeys, good and bad, and let's not forget the fun.

DEDICATION

I dedicate this book In memory of the people I loved and lost but mostly to the people who deal with the memory of and current abuse I always say never let an abuser control your life take control and if your the abuser reading this book please stop your abuse and seek help there are so many programs and people who are willing to lend an ear and shoulder you need to control yourself and understand the hurt you are causing not only to your victim but to yourself

CHAPTER 1

The 1960s was a decade of violence where we came so close in 1962 to starting World War III, which could have ended this world in nuclear annihilation. If President Kennedy would not made an exchange with the Soviet Union to pull our nuclear missiles out of Turkey and the Soviet Union would remove theirs from Cuba. We would have started a war that would have changed everything about the world we know today. The decade also brought us the Vietnam War, which brought the anti-war protests.

It was a time of civil rights ranging from women's rights to equal employment, taking them from housewives to working mothers. Minorities were also fighting for their rights, even though slavery had ended over a hundred years ago. The Blacks were still treated as if they didn't deserve the same rights as the whites. The Hispanics didn't fare much better even though a good percentage were American citizens; they feared deportation almost every day.

President John F. Kennedy was assassinated in the streets of Dallas, Texas, in 1963, and his brother Robert nearly five years later. It has left our country wondering why these two brothers shared the same fate. I personally believe it was because the two wanted the same thing. To make serious changes in our government. If their assassinations had never taken place, I believe our country would be very different. Even though many witnesses say, gunshots were fired from other areas, with the proof that the lone gunman theory was not how it happened. A man named Jim Garrison was the only prosecutor who ever made a case in Kennedy's murder and tried proving a man named Clay Shaw was, in fact, a CIA operative who had knowledge of how and who killed our president. Clay Shaw was found not guilty due to no proof of him being in the CIA. In 2003, the CIA released documents proving Clay Shaw received an initial five agency clearance on March 23, 1949. With no proof, the lone gunman shooting from the rear is how President Kennedy was killed. People to this day, over fifty years later, want the real truth.

They say the 60s was one of the most memorable decades in US History. There were six political assassinations between 1963 and 1968. So many people were trying to find out who they were with free love and Rock and Roll music. The Beatles to Elvis Presley were rocking out the radio stations driving women of all ages crazy. Sex, drugs, and rock and roll were the way. I was born nearly dead in the middle of it all. On June 10, 1966, My parents borrowed a car to head to Hurley Hospital. With the rain and thunder, my father had to drive with his head hanging out the window. Because the car they borrowed had no wipers. Hurley Hospital was in Buick City (also known as) Flint, Michigan, which had the largest manufacturing plant in the world. Hurley was considered to have the best pediatrics and burn unit in the country. My grandfather on my mother's side experienced firsthand when my mother was a young girl. He was trying to thaw frozen water pipes in the basement when a gas leak caused an explosion. With fourth-degree burns, he burned over thirty-five percent of his body, including his face and hands. He was never the same.

Hurley Hospital was named after James Hurley, who donated fifty-five thousand dollars and a chunk of land in memory of his wife, Mary, who died of a serious illness in 1900. Sadly the hospital did not open until 1908, three years after James's death.

I mention the pediatric unit's reputation because when my mother was just over five months pregnant. She lost her balance one morning, heading to the restroom and reaching out to break her fall. She pulled an ironing table on top of her resulting in a near miscarriage and losing a significant amount of blood and amniotic fluid, causing me to have very dry skin at birth. In the early hours of June 10, 1966, my mother gave birth to me at this particular hospital. I weighed just over four pounds. My skin was so dry it seemed I had scales from being in the womb with not enough amniotic fluid to keep my skin hydrated. Don't worry; I no longer look like a fish!! It did cause me some problems. I was given a lotion bath three times a day in my first couple of months. And because of my weight, I was at a huge risk of health problems.

As a young boy, the dry skin issue caused me many problems. Just before my fingernails, my fingers would crack, and the skin peeled back sometimes with bleeding; the pain was constant. Also, the bottom of my feet would be so dry they would crack badly, and it looked like my feet had a severe earthquake. I had to soak them in Epsom salt and rub the prescribed lotion nearly every day. Even sometimes wrapping my feet with gauze. As you can imagine, it was not very much fun. Out in the waiting room stood my father, waiting to hear the news about whether I was a boy or a girl. In those days, doctors weren't able to tell the sex of the baby until he or she was born. It was always a surprise. Since I barely weighed four pounds, I wasn't able to go home right away. I had to gain a few pounds. I was placed into an incubator to free me from any germs; getting sick could end my life. As my father was leaving the hospital, my mother noticed he jumped up and kicked his heels. Little did she know what sort of future was in store for us. I am not saying I don't have some good memories. But my father left horrible memories for my mom, sister, and me.

CHAPTER 2

I spent my first four to five months zipped up in my mother's leather coat. Riding on the back of our motorcycle to get around since my parents did not own a car. Right from the start, it seemed my life was going to be very interesting. As I got bigger, it got harder just to zip me up. My parents had to break down and finally buy a car. Until they were able to purchase a car, I was babysat by two sisters, Joan and Marie. They were daughters of some friends my parents knew. I didn't know their parents at all; I was in my teens before meeting their mother, who never seemed to like me for some reason. The sisters were constantly in and out. Sometimes, they would be there for a week or two, then gone for a month or so, and then show back up.

I never really understood who they were, but they always referred to me as their little brother. In the first year of my life, my parents spent time moving around here and there and even spent time somewhere in Missouri. Late in 1967, this sicko out of the California area. Charles Manson convinced over one hundred people that he was the Messiah. He had nearly one hundred people living in the San Fernando area at the Spahn Ranch. Following his commands, he turned the women into his sex toys. He talked his followers into committing some of the worst brutal murders in history. He even had a fourteen-year-old girl who he was sexually assaulting and brainwashing.

He kidnapped his own friend, torturing him for days before stabbing him to death. All because he thought he was some great musician and no one could see it but him. Manson and his followers came to an end after going on a killing spree. In August of 1969, when his group of sickos murdered a beautiful actress. Who was about to become a mother, stabbing her sixteen times, cutting off one of her breasts, and even removing her unborn child. They even killed the pizza delivery man outside before going into the house. Where they tortured and cut her friends to pieces right in front of her before turning on her. I think anyone sick enough to do these sorts of things should be put to death. Anyone who can commit a crime so awful is capable of anything. They do not deserve the right even to breathe.

For most of my early childhood, we lived in a house my grandparents owned in the Beecher community (outside of Flint, Michigan). They owned two homes right next door to one another.

I spent many weekends with them. I remember one-morning eating breakfast, my grandma was picking up something off the floor, and my grandpa reached over and swatted her on the rear, saying, "Good job, woman." He then told me, "Ya gotta keep your woman on her toes to make sure she keeps a clean house. You have to give them a good swat on the rear once in a while."

I thought, *Wow, really! I need to remember that.* Guys, take this advice, don't try it with women nowadays; you're liable to wake up in the hospital!

My grandfather owned several properties, including a few apartments and a church, which had a house behind it, where my grandma lived right after they split up. Personally, I don't have a lot of memories of the place. I do recall my father being dropped off there after getting out of jail. He was pretty abusive. Even at that age, So I wasn't very happy to see him.

My mom told me when I was around three, I was at the table being a brat, not wanting to eat, and my dad started screaming at me. He threw a spoon catching me in the corner of my eye, causing my eye to bleed quite badly. My mother was so angry she wanted to do the same to him. As I got older, the abuse got worse. Experts say there are four types of abuse, some more severe than others; physical, sexual, neglect, and emotional, and he wasn't shy about giving all four. He also shared the abuse with my mom. He would physically punch her and put her down. He was no one to throw stones, as he never graduated. My mother had gone to college to graduate with a bachelor's, becoming a schoolteacher.

My grandparents used to pick me up every Sunday morning for church. My grandfather had been a reverend since my mother was young. I would stand on the couch looking out the front window, which took up most of the front wall facing the driveway. I wasn't quite able to say grandpa, so I called him Boppa. As I looked out the window, I would repeat Boppa until they pulled in the drive. Then I would run to the door screaming, "Boppa! Boppa!" in excitement.

When I was about two years old, my parents became friends with a couple from my grandpa's church. After a while of them being friends, I was told to call them Uncle Bob and Aunt Shirley. As they got to know each other, Bob decided to introduce my parents to an outlaw bike club. It was hush-hush at first, but then we started having biker parties. We would have bonfires and keg parties even though it was against the law to have fires in the neighborhood. We were never bothered by the cops. I can remember waking up the following morning to the house smelling like beer and cigarettes; bikers were sleeping everywhere, and some had cigarettes still lit in their mouths.

The bikers liked teaching me how to fight. Never let anyone take the first punch; they said always aim for the nose. No matter how big someone is, if you hit the nose hard enough, they will go down. Then, you just kick the shit out of them. One particular member they called Sugar Tit because all he talked about was tits. How he loved sucking on titties, big tits, little tits, didn't matter to him. He taught me to fake with the left, then hit with the right as hard as you can right in the nose. One night we were boxing; I faked him and missed his nose but caught him right in the eye as hard as I could. His eye immediately started watering up. He wound up with one hell of a black eye. As you can imagine, that's not one bikers let you live down.

That's when they started calling me Little Ponch. They would pat me on the back and call me a little badass, especially when later the club discovered he was an undercover cop. The President gave me my own cut (aka) a vest with the club name on the back and my name on the front. One thing people should know about bikers in general. Even though most of them look like something that crawled out from under a rock, mostly good-hearted people, they always seemed to have a special place for kids. These guys took a liking to me. I felt these guys cared for me more than my own father. They wouldn't do anything intentionally to cause harm to kids. At least the majority of them, some of them just don't give a shit about who gets hurt. There are rules most of them live by; if you break them, depending on what you do, it matters as to what kind of punishment you receive.

I've witnessed some of these punishments firsthand, and believe me when I say they are not fun to watch. Most of the time, they just receive a beat down, some are more severe than others, and the more severe ones were usually carried out in the club barn. Some were worse than a beatdown. Some were never seen again, meaning they were either kicked from the club or killed. I only know of one or two—some of the beatdowns I've seen happen during parties. My aunt and I watched one on our front porch. There was a window in the living room where you could see the front porch. A member called Gino was getting a severe beating. When I started crying because Gino was one of my favorites, and watching him get beat was upsetting. My mom saw us standing there watching, so she went and told Cuddles. I was watching and crying. Lucky for Gino, they stopped kicking his ass. Cuddles was the club president. He got his name because he was a huge badass guy whose ole lady said he was just a big cuddly bear. He hated the name, so we just shortened it to Cuddles. After Gino came into the house, I recall trying to help clean him up, but he said to leave him alone. I just let him be. Not only does a beating hurt like hell, but it's also embarrassing, especially when people are watching or when a kid tries to clean you up.

CHAPTER 3

We actually had been in two separate clubs. Before transitioning from the first to the second club, my dad decided to try to join a much larger club known in California with many chapters; the meeting obviously did not go very well for him. When he came home from the meeting, he had three cracked ribs and a broken nose; also, he was covered in blood. Needless to say, he never contacted that club again.

I don't have many memories of the first club except for Uncle Bob, who was vice president, and the president, whose real name was also Bob. His nickname was Crabs; his wife nicknamed him because she said he was always digging at his balls like he had crabs. Uncle Bob also got a great name, Anus, because people were always saying what an asshole. Some guys got other weird names like Sugar Tit was another. My dad, I think, got a good one. They called him Poncho because he was always wearing one. We even had a guy called Magilla because he had extremely long arms and could almost scratch his knees standing straight up. He had bright red hair and a beard which hung down to his belly. I would hold onto his beard, and he would lift me up and swing me back and forth. I thought he was the coolest guy.

Once in a while, my mother would get fed up and try leaving my father. We would move into an apartment somewhere. We would have to walk to the store for groceries or maybe to a restaurant, taking the bus to doctor appointments. She would get lonely sometimes and cry. I did my best to comfort her but still did not tell her of the abuse. I think somehow, I was not only afraid to tell but also embarrassed. I knew eventually we would be living with him again and feared what he might do if she was to tell him. Sometimes she would invite a few members over to hang out. Have a few beers, smoke a little weed, and listen to music—anything to clear the mind.

My mother told me about a time. I came running out of the bathroom screaming. One of the ole ladies caught me and helped me out. It seems I caught my peter in the zipper, YOWW! Funny, I don't remember. How could a guy not remember catching his peter in a zipper? It seems to me that would stick.

Right around the time, we were joining the first club. Our country was about to jump into a big change of its own. In 1968 four days before I turned two, Robert Kennedy was assassinated in Los Angeles, California. After just winning primary elections in California and South Dakota. Almost two months after, a man named Dr. Martin Luther King Jr, a minister who was fighting for equal rights. Not just for black people but for every race, he was assassinated in Memphis, Tennessee April 3, 1968. His death prompted the worst racial riots in history all across the country. Causing major property damages in more than one hundred cities and multiple deaths everywhere. Blood not only covered the streets, but our government was fighting amongst itself. Not just over Vietnam and the riots, but were also having some difficulty with North Korea. It was a bad year for the whole country.

I remember one morning when I was about five; my father took me into his room. *My first thought was, why are we here?* He told me he wanted to stick his penis in my mouth. I thought *how gross; I was confused about why he would want to do this to me.* Fathers are not supposed to do this to their children. He made me get down on my knees and tried forcing it down my throat. I began choking, nearly puking. As I started to cry, he stood me up and then forced my face down on the bed, where he tried to penetrate me from behind. Even as I cried, he abused me no matter what I said. I couldn't understand why he was doing this to me. Once he was finished, he told me not to cry or tell anyone because no one would believe me anyway, and the next time it would be worse. This abuse continued and got worse as I got older.

I had never seen a black person in my neighborhood until I was around eight years old, walking down my street. I thought to myself; they are in the wrong area. As I started going to school, there were more and more. By the time I got to junior high school, there were more of them than there were of the whites. I had made friends with a few black kids when I was in elementary. We used to beat on our desks and dance around like fools whenever the teacher was out. We would wrestle and have fun. I would get dirty looks from the white kids who were prejudiced because of their parents. My mom was friends with a white lady who had mixed kids, which at the time was unheard of. Her friend got a lot of harassment from the neighbors and other whites. I wasn't too bothered by it because the father was never around. I didn't have to watch them kiss or anything. I hung out with her son Junior. He and I were always getting into something.

One time we were jumping around on a broken-down car, and I fell off and hit my head on a piece of metal. Wound up with eight stitches. One summer, when I was nine, I broke my arm. I was climbing a tree with Joan. I lost my footing, caught my arm between two branches, and dislocated my elbow. It turned completely around. I could literally see the elbow of my right arm. There were a few guys from the club over-drinking beer. I started running towards the house, screaming. Cuddles was standing there with a couple of other guys who saw me running, noticed the elbow, and ran after me. I think he was as freaked out as I was. Cuddles and a few other guys followed us to the hospital. I didn't even have to wait; as soon as the nurse saw me, she ran me right to the back. As the doctor was trying to relocate my arm, I was screaming quite a bit, as you can imagine. It hurt like hell!

The club guys could hear me screaming and were getting pissed off. Cuddles ran down the hall and told the doctor. If they heard me scream one more time, he was going to be doing some screaming of his own. I'm not sure what happened then. I either passed out, or he tranquilized me because I woke up with a cast on my arm, and I was in some sort of caged hospital bed, which kind of freaked me out. Like was I in jail or something? I guess it was to keep me from climbing out of bed or falling out. I wore a cast for six weeks and a partial for another six. The doctor told my parents I would never use my right arm correctly again, and I would always have difficulty using it.

I was stuck there for nearly a week. I believe it was the first time I got homesick. When my parents would come to visit, I could hear them coming down the hall. I could hear the sound of the cuts because they had chains and buttons. I also heard the cowboy boots and remember crying when they left. *I never understood why. Why in the hell would I wanna go home?* I think it was mainly because I was bored to death. It does seem to me that for some reason, children who are abused by a parent, or even both parents, still somehow love them. After I broke my arm, my relationship with my father changed. I couldn't quite figure out why, but hey, he wasn't hurting me anymore. My father started wrestling with me, tickling me, acting like a real dad. We even started fishing together; at first, I was scared of him molesting me while fishing. After a while, I got more comfortable. One time we started talking with another guy who was just about to leave. He caught a big mouth bass and was going to toss it. He had to go to work, and one fish wasn't going to do it, so my dad said, "Hey, we'll take it." We fished all morning and caught some bluegill but no bass. As we were driving home, my dad said, "Hey, let's tell mom you caught that fish."

At first, I thought, okay, but then my mom started to take pictures. I thought for sure he would wind up telling my mom the truth. I was totally embarrassed; I was getting pictures with a fish I didn't catch. I knew he told fibs now and again, but this was a little weird. I didn't want to rock the boat by telling my mom the truth. I guess sometimes you start noticing things about people once the cat is out of the bag. I noticed all the stories he would tell, so I nicknamed him Father Goose because he told so many stories that it was hard to know whether he was storytelling or telling the truth. I found myself waking up some mornings listening to him sitting in the kitchen. He would be storytelling to whoever was there. I would get up to sit and listen. It was actually entertaining. I got to the point of being able to tell when he was storytelling or telling the truth. As I grew older, I had the gift of knowing when people were telling me a story or not.

CHAPTER 4

I used to put toys and stuff behind my bedroom door. That way, I would hear someone coming in. I wish people who abuse their children would understand what this is doing to them. They don't just wake up the next day, forget, and go on as if nothing happened. A piece of them die every time. Not only do they not forget, but they're also no longer the same child. They become someone else. As they grow older, they find themselves crying for no reason or lashing out in anger, mostly at the ones they love most. Some relive the abuse every day, and others are lucky enough to put it away. Society has become more aware of what this abuse does to children. Research has shown one hundred percent of serial killers have been abused in one way or another. I personally believe most of them have been sexually abused. Sexual and emotional abuse will cause most children to lock themselves away, and some even commit suicide, luckily. Not everyone who is abused goes down the path of being a murderer or committing suicide. They all go through their own pain and torment. It sometimes feels as if you're in a boxed room where all four sides have something trying to harm you; with no door, there's no way out.

Early one year, I was sleeping on the couch during a party. A prospect (AKA) is someone who hangs out with the club but is not a member. Picked up a toy gun and put it to my head as if to shoot me. Magilla saw him do this, grabbed him up, and beat the living shit out of him. My mother said she had to stop him before he killed the guy as he hung him on a hook screwed into the wall. He told me he would kill him if he ever came near me again. I'm sure you can guess he was never seen again.

We had another prospect whose nickname was Shakey because he was a huge Elvis fan. He would shake his knees singing to an Elvis record. When I got older, I found out Shakey had spent most of his life in a state hospital before joining the club. He stayed at my house for long periods. We sort of adopted him; he had no family we knew of, and we became the only family he ever had. One night, we all went to a party in the woods. Where they tied a rope around the branch of a tree that hung out over the water, these drunken fools would swing out and jump into the water. Some not know how to swim.

What dumb asses, if you can't swim, don't jump. A few of these idiots would swing out, not letting go. And on the swing back. WHAM! Right into the side of the hill. Ow, that had to hurt. Watching these idiots was like watching a comedy show as they're trying to climb the hill coming back up. Oops, lost their footing and fell back to the bottom. Do these guys not realize they were too old and too drunk to be doing this kind of stuff? Especially in the dark, someone could have killed themselves. With the bonfires, guys fighting, and keg chugging where someone would be held upside down and drinking as much as possible from the keg before nearly drowning themselves was fun to watch. They would get up and stagger around before falling and puking. One night my parents and I had left a bit early, but Shakey wanted to stay; against better judgment, my parents agreed. Since Shakey has spent most of his life in a state hospital, he wasn't much of a drinker. He hadn't drunk any alcohol since God knows when. He got totally drunk. One of those kinds where you wake up the next morning thinking. What the fuck happened to me last night? What happened was he hallucinated, thinking one of the member's ole lady was the devil, and literally threw her into the fire! Luckily, another member was standing close by, saw what was happening, and jumped in after her. He managed to get them both out without too many burns. Shakey, on the other hand, received the beating of his life. Uncle Bob kept him from being killed and brought him home to our house. To say the least, he definitely was confused the following morning, waking up with black eyes, among other injuries.

Since my grandfather owned some properties, even some apartments, he was into carpentry, wiring, and building, you name it. He actually built the house they were living in. He bought some land in Clio and decided to build a house. Besides being a minister, he was also a licensed barber. He worked at a few shops here and there but decided he wanted his own shop. He bought a carnival vending trailer and put it at the front of his land, built a foundation, and turned the trailer into a barbershop. My grandpa was very talented and considered an intelligent man among his peers until he decided to move my father's younger sister into the home.

Talk about a disaster. Never move a younger woman into your house when you're a married man. Especially if she's single because there's no happy ending in a situation like that; as you can imagine, he wound up cheating on my grandma and got my aunt pregnant. I'm not sure exactly how that was explained. Since my aunt didn't know anyone except the folks at the church, she had no license also no such thing as a computer. At first, the father had to be a mystery until my grandma found out somehow. My grandpa was the father. She wound up divorcing him. She refused to stay with anyone who could cheat, especially a minister. Not only did he lose his wife, but also the respect of his peers, who forced him to give up his ministry. Not to mention the respect of his family. My grandmother moved into the house behind the church. Then eventually moved into the house next door to us after the divorce. He was forced to give my grandmother some of the properties. Since I was too young to understand what was happening and why my grandparents were living separately. No one told me about the divorce. Or my cousin was my grandpa's son.

After my parents explained the situation, I asked my mom, "How can he do that if he's a preacher? Won't God punish him?" Well, believe me, he was punished alright, being married to a mentally disabled woman. Imagine the kids they had. Not to mention my mom believes she cheated on him as well. If she's willing to have sex with a married man, then she's willing to cheat. That's the one thing I don't understand about religion; Baptist, Catholic. There are so many types of religion. I sure can't name them all, but cheating on your spouse and molesting children are frowned upon no matter what your religion; yet people are constantly cheating, priests are molesting children, or people are murdering other people in the name of their religion. I mean, if I was God, I think I would end it all. *What are people thinking? Do they not read the Bible? And if they do, how is it that they don't believe in what they are reading?* People claim they do, yet they break every law they can. At least when it comes to their religion. If they break human law, they go to jail or have some type of consequence. They break the Bible's law, and all they do is say, I'm sorry. Please forgive me and then go on as if nothing happened. The Bible even says men being with men or women being with women is against God's law, but as a society now, everyone views it as normal. Even having a gay month, I'm getting sick just thinking about it.

CHAPTER 5

I was happy having my grandma next door as I got to eat all the cherries I wanted. She had two cherry trees in front of the house. My buddy Turner and I ate so many cherries we almost turned into one. We also thought the sap on the trees was honey. Turner and I would try and chew it off. Luckily, our teeth weren't strong enough. *Yuck, can you imagine?* Having my grandma, next door was great. She was always baking something or cutting up watermelons. One weird thing. She had no backyard; there was only maybe a foot or two between the house and the fence for the neighbor behind her. They say it's amazing that kids in my era survived everything we did, like drinking water out of the hose. The rough playing we did on our bikes and jumping off things. Especially at the playground, there was always one way or another to break our necks. We never had to go indoors until the streetlights came on. We were always fighting with one kid or another from the neighborhood but never had to worry about the cops showing up at your door. Most of us just took or dished out the ass-whipping. If we lost, we just made sure to fight harder next time.

My friends and I would jump the fence behind my grandma's house to get at the neighbor's grape vines. We got caught a few times, and when the guy figured out who we were. He came around the corner and told my parents. It wasn't like nowadays, where you might get a timeout.

Oh, I got a time out, alright. From being able to sit down because my butt hurt, too bad. We just had to be a little more careful to avoid getting caught next time. We used a lookout, and the rest snagged grapes. Between those grapes, my grandma's cherry trees, and the other fruit trees in the neighborhood, we were never hungry. She told us we could have all the cherries she wasn't able to reach. The ones she was able to pick she made into cherry pies, yummy! Those were the days when we actually played outside! Which was way more fun than being inside, even though we would get yelled at sometimes for eating their fruit. We would just run off and come back later. We had this little store on the corner a couple of blocks away. We would spend every dime we had there. They had the widest variety of candy you ever saw. I mean Sweet n Sour suckers, lemon heads, Boston Baked beans. You name it; he had it. This guy who owned the store was the meanest grouch. He would stand there, "Hurry up, pick what you want. I ain't got all day." Man, did we hate that guy. Since he was bald, we nicknamed him "Meathead," and the store was called Meathead's Market. We never talked back to the adults, though; we knew better. Some of them even had permission to punish us. It really sucked getting a whipping from someone else other than your parents. When I was around eight, there was a vacant lot across the street from our driveway, and our house sat on a hill. Our driveway was pretty steep. A few of us kids were riding our bikes down the driveway into the vacant lot across the street to see who could go the farthest without pedaling. When it was my turn, I didn't notice a white car coming. Since we were in a residential neighborhood, he should have been driving a bit slower. He was also not paying attention because he had no license due to having a DUI and was running from being pulled over. Before I knew it, I was flying through the air. As I was falling onto his hood, it seemed as if time had slowed down. I was able to look him right in the eyes. It looked as if they were going to pop out of his head. By the time he stopped, we were in front of my grandma's driveway next door. I flew off the hood and immediately scrambled behind this huge boulder. Scared to death, then I could hear my mom screaming. Then a few club members were screaming at the guy behind the wheel. Bad enough, he had just hit a kid, but a kid who belonged to an outlaw club, and the fact he was a black guy didn't help. At the time, blacks were not welcome in our area. He was quite scared himself, with a bunch of bikers trying to get his door open. Then someone screamed. I was under the car. It was all happening so fast. As they were looking under the car, I stood up. My mom immediately grabbed me and started looking me over to see if I was okay. Other than a few scrapes, my right ankle was the only thing really injured. As soon as everyone's attention was on me, the driver quickly took off. As I have mentioned, people were not in the habit of calling the police every time something happened. Of course, the members decided to look for the driver themselves. I hate to think about what may have happened to the driver if they were to find him. The following day a lady came to the house, claiming it was her husband who had hit me and that he had been worried about my well-being. She mentioned she came by a few hours after the accident, but we were at the hospital. I feel *what kind of man sends his wife to do the job he should have done.* Did he not think she could have been beaten by a bunch of angry bikers? I mean, what an asshole. I can't believe my parents didn't call the cops. Who's to say he won't kill the next kid he hits? Had he not been a drunk driver, this would have never happened. I also believe the damage to my ankle was the real cause of my knee popping out later on in life. After my grandpa remarried, I recall one day during a visit, I looked around the house and said, "What's going on here? Was grandma not on her toes? I think you need to give Aunt Berta a good swatting a little more often. This house looks terrible." *It smelled terrible too,* I thought to myself. Especially my cousin's room which smelled like he had forgotten where the toilet was.

One day some guy came over asking my dad to cut up a motorcycle, and like an idiot, he agreed after spending days cutting this thing up, removing all the usable parts. He was visited by a few detectives, telling him he was under arrest for destroying stolen goods. They were even going to arrest my mom, but the judge said, "We can't be putting mothers in jail." *Nowadays, mom or not, you're going to jail.* After leaving the first club, Crabs started building these awesome-looking three-wheelers made out of old Volkswagen beetles. He would cut the body off, weld the front end of a motorcycle on the front of the beetle, and make leather seats with a top. They were so cool-looking. He would put them in car shows which I got to go to quite often. Which was the first time I saw the Batmobile.

Living that kind of childhood was very confusing for me, as it would be for any child. I would spend a week or so with my grandparents before starting school. Talking about going from one kind of life to another was definitely weird. After my grandparents divorced, my sister and I started attending a different church with my grandma. Her family had been friends with the reverend and his family since she was a small girl. We knew the family quite well. My sister and I got really close to them. It was very sad losing them when they passed. They were the most loving people I've ever known. The younger reverend and his wife ran the Boy Scouts, which I was a part of. I had so much fun being a part of it with camping, canoeing, and fishing. The fun was endless until it was time to go home. There was this one kid who went to church. He had been adopted by one of the family members. His name was McCall; talk about a little bastard. He would pick on my sister and other kids smaller than him, and then when I would go after him. Somehow, he would always get to his parents before I could get my hands on him. I wanted to kick his little ass so bad. Later on, during our teens, we became good friends and had a lot of fun.

CHAPTER 6

Neighborhoods, in general, were just so different. As I said, kids played outside back then, and boy, did we have a lot of fun. We used to hang out riding our bikes. We would build camps and tree houses. There was always something to do, even in the winter.

We had these two brothers who liked riding bikes with us. Sometimes there were too many guys and not enough bikes. Depending on the seats, some would ride on the back, but mostly on the handlebars. They had to be careful not to catch their feet in the spokes. Which not only hurt like hell but would flip the bike and hurt both of you. One day we found a great jumping spot right at the end of a driveway. There was a little hill with a church dirt parking lot right behind the hill, and the way the street passed the drive, you could ride as fast as possible, hit the hill, and fly! I mean, you could really get a great jump. We had to have a lookout for the crossing street to make sure no cars were coming. The younger of the two brothers was taking his turn, and boy, was he really moving when he hit the hill. I think he broke a record; as he hit his peak of flight, the front tire of his bike went flying off. It seemed as if time somehow slowed down. We could only watch in horror as we all started yelling, "OOHH NOO!" You could even see the look on his face as he came down onto the parking lot. His forks stabbed right into the dirt parking lot, slamming his face into the handlebars, and he flew across the parking lot.

We just stood and looked at each other, thinking, *holy shit, he's dead!* He got up crying, blood on his forehead, his nose bleeding, he had dirt in his hair, he was just messed up! He was our pal, so we all walked him home after collecting his tire on the other side of the busy main street and getting his forks out of the parking lot. Believe it or not, they weren't even damaged. We put his tire back on and explained to his mother what had happened. Of course, she didn't believe us. She thought we beat him up and said, "He won't be playing with you anymore." He had to start sneaking away to hang out. Eventually, he just hung out less and less. Turner had a cousin who would sometimes visit and hang out with us. We decided to go and jump off my garage. Because there was a tree on the left side close enough, we would climb the tree and get onto the garage. Well, I had jumped off other roofs before, but every time I landed, my ankles would sting.

Turner suggested when I land to just fall to the ground and roll. I thought, cool, okay. He said, "Watch." He did it and had no pain in his ankles. Great! I jumped and did what he said, and with no pain. Allen took his turn, and then it was Steve's turn. In those days, not everyone had a dryer, so my mom used to hang our clothes out on a line. My dad had screwed these hooks into the side of the garage to tie the line too. It just so happened my parents purchased a dryer a few months back, so we didn't need the line anymore but never removed the hooks. *See what's about to happen?*

As Steve was hanging his feet over the edge, the front of the shoe snagged a hook. He said, "See, it ain't hard. Watch." He attempted to make his jump. Instead, he did an upside-down kind of jump. Since he was sort of a chubby kid, he slammed into the side of the garage with a significant amount of force. He was hanging upside down, crying for us to help him. It was a bit hard to do because he was pretty heavy. We couldn't reach the hook, and besides, we couldn't stop laughing. It was the funniest thing I'd have ever seen. Steve went home the next morning, and we didn't see him again either. Not for a long time. It seemed we were having problems keeping friends. We couldn't figure out why, lol. We also did not jump off the garage again until those hooks were gone.

The sixties and seventies were two decades of political and civil violence. Even as a kid, I had my own demons to live with. The seventies had left me with horrible memories. It took many years to finally come to terms with the abuse I suffered. My father was a sick man who was not only physically abusive but emotionally abusive. Not only to me but to my mom as well. Mainly because she would defend me; as I got older, I would try defending her by fighting him, even though a little boy stood no chance against a full-grown man. I did the best I could.

I remember when I was about ten years old, my dad was fighting with my mom, and he had her on the floor, hitting her. My sister and I had paddles we would get our swats from when we were in trouble. They were hanging on the wall. I tried physically pulling him off but was unable to. There was even a couple who was just standing there watching. I yelled at them, "Why don't you help her?"

People during those times just stayed out of shit. I saw the paddle on the wall, grabbed it, and started to hit my dad. Hoping it would hurt him. Instead, it just pissed him off, so he turned on me. I fought as hard as I could until my mom got up.

Then she threw herself between my dad and me, yelling, "Don't you dare hit him for protecting his mother. He's got every right to protect his mom" She wound up punching him in the face. As he backed off, that proved to me he was a coward. It was the first time she had actually fought back.

I had taken beatings for my mom and my sister, but it wasn't the worst abuse nor the emotional. The worst abuse I ever suffered was the sexual. When my little sister was old enough, I would intercept him from hurting her. As time passed, I became stronger as he abused me. I would quietly scream and cry inside so he wouldn't know how badly I hurt. It was my way of showing I was stronger than him. Many nights I would cry myself to sleep. I couldn't allow him to hurt my little sister. I was her big brother. It was my job to protect her. I have always been protective of people who are not able to defend themselves. I've received many beatings, not only from my father. I even tried a few times to protect some of the ole ladies from the club. In the early 1970s, we had been pulling troops from Vietnam due to a lack of public support and the fact this was a war we had never fought before. Guerrilla warfare was something we were not prepared for. Nearly two thousand Americans were left there; about eight hundred have been recovered through the years. Still, over fifteen hundred have yet to be found. This particular war has left a hole in so many people's lives. I had a conversation once with a vet who told me stories that kept him up at night. He told me about the first night he was in Vietnam. His job was to walk back and forth on a dock; every third time, he was to shoot a flare over the water to light up the area. He said his third time shooting the flare, "I had never seen so many people walking along the shoreline." He was only eighteen at the time he said, "It scared the living shit out of me."

Other stories like a Vietnamese woman had injured a soldier by inserting a razor blade in her vagina, causing the soldier to nearly split his penis in half. They tortured the woman for days. They were cutting her with razor blades all over her body. Pouring gas on her, setting her on fire, putting the fire out before killing her. He said, "I can still hear her screaming." He wound up passing away with a bottle of liquor in his hand. What those men went through was horrible. Like my friend, some were barely old enough to have ever been with a woman.

CHAPTER 7

I can remember the last time my father sexually abused me as if it was yesterday. We were going to a car show the next morning, and I believed the sexual abuse was over. Because he hadn't hurt me that way in quite a while. I quit putting things behind my door. I woke up to him being behind me, taking off my pajamas. I asked him, "Please don't." His reply was, "You wanna go to the car show, right?" I was twelve years old. As I went through this abuse, I always tried to picture myself somewhere else. Somewhere where I wasn't being hurt. Children are scared to say anything mainly because they think people won't believe them and possibly say something to the abuser. The abuser will then hurt them even worse, or maybe the abuser would take out their anger on a loved one. Children always want to protect the people they love.

I had started putting things behind my door again. Until I moved into a different section of the house where there wasn't as much privacy as a bedroom, he wouldn't feel safe abusing me there as there was more chance of being caught by someone. It took a very long time for me to sleep without nightmares. I had one recurring nightmare. In this dream, I was being chased by a monster, and my legs felt like rubber. I would keep falling and would look behind me to see the monster gaining on me. I could never make out what the monster looked like. I just knew I was terrified. I managed to find a mechanic shop and get on the roof. As I walked backward, waiting to see if I had lost him, I tripped and fell off the roof. As I was falling, the monster was standing in the bed of a pickup truck, reaching to catch me. I would then wake up with my heart racing and dripping with sweat. *Looking back, I think the monster was my father.* I felt in my heart there was no escape. Some nights I would daydream I was living as someone else with a family who loved and respected me. When *it comes down to it, isn't that what we all want our families to do Love and respect us?*

My sister and I had a strange relationship. I tried protecting her from my father since she was little, and obviously, I couldn't protect her every day. I felt I had failed her so many times. I don't think she really knows all the times I took the abuse meant for her. I think it's why she and I weren't as close as we should have been. She had always been my dad's favorite, along with my grandparents, which upset me quite a bit because I had always been close to both my grandparents. Once she was old enough to start spending the night or weekend with them. She was who they asked for. I was no longer as important. So I began to reject her. I couldn't understand why they loved her more. I hadn't changed; I was still their grandson. *Why didn't they want me anymore?* I felt we no longer had the closeness we once shared. But we were always protective of each other growing up, even though we fought a lot. It's something all siblings do. After I got older, my mom told me she had to tell my grandparents. If they couldn't love me the same, don't bother, you won't see either one. I felt as if I had been stabbed in the heart to think she would have to actually say that. It was something my mom should not have told me. I don't think she knew how much it hurt me. I have never felt the same about them since.

After my father molested me for the last time when I was twelve, I woke up a couple of weeks later being punched. I fell out of bed, trying to get away as he was kicking me. He was screaming the whole time about my dog being stuck under the car. I believed he was angrier about the fact I moved my sleeping quarters. I hurried outside to get my dog, trying to keep the blood out of my eyes. My dog's chain was stuck under the tire after I freed him and chained him back to his doghouse. I had to take a bath and clean myself up before going to work, which I was already late. All I could do was cry, sitting in the tub watching the bath water as it turned red from the blood. Showing up to work with marks on my face and having to lie about what happened was getting old. It was time to start fighting back.

One year, when I was about fourteen, my parents got a call from someone claiming to be my dad's older sister. Barb had found us; she had been searching for quite some time and finally found her original family. After she saw what she found, she soon regretted it. The truth became more than she could bear; she eventually stayed away. Just as my Aunt Florie did, the friends she worked with at the hospital wanted to protect her from such a messed-up clan. My Grandmother Rose had been in an old folks' home for nearly a year. About the time Barb came around, we got a call from the hospital saying she had been thrown from a three-story window and had broken her hip and other injuries. She was asking to see my dad. I now know that my mom had to talk him into going for good reasons. I didn't know then she also wanted to see my sister and me. She talked about my father as a child, saying she regretted what had happened and that he had always been a good boy who cared for his younger sisters. She wanted to try and make amends for her actions. My Aunt Berta and grandpa took her in and cared for her. Barb did get to meet her and talk, but a few weeks later, she died. My Aunt Berta had all my grandmother's belongings and did not want to give anyone anything my dad and aunts were asking from her. Aunt Berta was not only a kleptomaniac; she was stingy as well.

It seemed I was losing my entire family because my aunts did not want to be around my father. I think because the abuse my sister and I suffered was now known by then. I don't think everyone knew to what extent the abuse went. I was now big enough to start fighting back. One morning not long after turning sixteen, my father was yelling at me because I had forgotten to feed my dog the night before. As I was making up a bowl of dog food, my dad said, "You don't have enough time to eat breakfast before going to school." I disagreed. By this time, I had no respect whatsoever for my dad, so I said, "I have enough time." We argued for a moment, and then he hit me upside the head, and that was all it took. We started fighting like cats and dogs. He got me in the eye just about the time I got a hold of the back of his neck.

I started pushing his face into the dirty sink water. My mom started yelling," You're going to drown him!" My first thought was, *Yup, that's the plan.* She made me let him go. Reluctantly, I let him go but not without a warning;

we weren't going to be putting up with his shit anymore. I went to school with a black eye from the fight. The next thing I knew, CPS was taking me from my parents. I wound up in a foster home for nearly two months, and when I returned to school, I got called into the principal's office. My first thought was, *Damn; I hadn't even been back for a day yet. What could I have done?* It turned out that I got too many unexcused absences. I told him I had been in a foster home because they called CPS. He wanted me to show some proof. I thought, *Seriously, you're the pricks who called them. Look it up, asshole.* I basically had an attitude about it and never went back.

One thing also makes me different from my father. I always had an idea of how to make money. I took after my grandfather. When I was seven, I came up with the idea of cleaning up pretty rocks, took my wagon down to the corner store, and sat out front selling rocks. I even pushed an ice cream cart when I was fifteen for about two summers, not making any money working all day. I hated that job didn't take long for me to quit. I had even delivered newspapers with a friend, and I kept the route even after he quit. I actually made decent money from the route. Back then, you had to be the one to collect the money from the customers, which I loved to do. There were these old folks who had been married for over seventy-five years. I would just sit and talk with them. I thought they were the nicest people on the planet. Some people I would just rather not deal with at all.

From the ages of twelve to seventeen, I went through a weird phase where I would be walking along, and out of nowhere, my knee would pop out of the socket. Mostly, it seemed to be my right knee, but again without any warning, my left knee would do the same. I would hit the floor in horrible pain. I've gone to the doctor and hospital a few times. No one could seem to figure out why my knee would pop out of the socket. It was hard to walk for a few days afterward. I remember the first time I was in class, and I was walking up to my teacher to go over my work, and whamo! I hit the floor screaming. It hurt so freaking bad I thought I broke my leg.

Another time, I was coming out of the grocery store, and I hit the ground again. It was my left knee this time. I spent a lot of time wearing a brace and walking with crutches. Sometimes it would go months without happening, and then sometimes, it would happen maybe twice a month. The worst time was when I was coming from my girlfriend's house, and it was pouring rain. I was running, jumping over a fence, and I fell to the ground screaming when I landed. My knee had popped completely out of place. I had to pop my knee back in. I had never felt this pain before. All I could do was lay there in the rain hoping someone would hear me. Luckily, the guy whose yard I was in heard me, came out, and carried me home. I never gave him a bit of shit after that. He only lived a few houses down, and I don't remember what I had done, but he had come to my place telling me not to do whatever it was I had been doing. He had a stuttering problem, and the asshole I was, I, started making fun of him. He should have kicked my ass, but the madder he got, the worse he stuttered. After he helped me that day, he became someone I looked up to. His wife and daughters started coming and hanging out with my parents. I came to really care for them all. It was a huge lesson for me.

Even though I had received many ass whippings as a kid, I also dished out a few ass whippings of my own. Especially since I was smaller, I never liked seeing smaller kids get picked on. My protective instinct would kick in, and I would wind up in a fight. My parents had friends whose kids would get picked on all the time and get beat up. I had to walk from my school to theirs and walk them home so no one would pick on them. Even though I was smaller than most, not too many kids had the balls to fuck with me. I had to kick a lot of ass to prove myself. A few times, my friends would basically sick me on the bullies because they weren't tough enough to do it themselves. I could sometimes be a bully, as I would hold kids to the ground. They weren't able to get free. I had one bully I was beating up and was holding him down. He wound up biting my balls, and I had to punch him in the head until he quit. I had a bite mark on my balls which hurt for nearly a week.

CHAPTER 8

I have many fun memories of the club, like when they would like to wrestle and box with me. Sometimes they would gang up on me. Stretching me out while members took turns tickling me. I've come so close to pissing myself many times. When they finally let me go, I would chase them around laughing. I sometimes still think of them and laugh. Then I have some scary and sad memories which will stick with me my whole life. Just about the time the Vietnam war was closing up. The club had a member who returned from the war as a different man. He was looking to take the club in a different direction and did not like Cuddles very well. He wanted to change everything about it. The name, some of its members, he wanted what they called a patch over, and he wanted Cuddles gone. But he wasn't able to get the vote he wanted. One day some of us were hanging at Cuddles when the phone rang. I could hear Cuddles in the back room yelling at whoever was on the phone. Next thing, my dad and Uncle Bob came running from the back. Saying we gotta get everyone in the back bedroom. As my mom is asking what was going on. all my dad would say was some bad people were on the way here. everyone is asking who? No answer as I'm watching my dad and Bob coming out of the front bedroom with shotguns. My mom and a few others shoved a dresser behind the door. It was obvious everyone should be lying on the floor. Everyone just stood there. Almost immediately, we heard some tires screeching out front and then yelling. The next thing was like being in a war. Suddenly, everyone hit the floor. Gunfire started; it was so loud I couldn't even hear the screaming. Almost as if they were being fired off in the house. It seemed as if it was never going to stop. Everyone was crying except me; I've heard gunfire many times. I was more curious than scared, wondering who was doing all the shooting. It stopped suddenly, and it got really quiet for a few minutes. Then some guys yelled for someone to open the door. Three women moved the dresser telling everyone to stay down. After opening the door, the women went toward the front room. Then suddenly, someone started yelling," OH, MY GOD!" Then I got a bit scared. I was curious to see what was happening. I opened the door slowly, and all I could see were people running around. Someone was on the couch, but I couldn't see who; too many people were standing in the way. I could see blood on the front door. There was also blood on the floor. The next thing I knew, my mom jerked the door open. Grabbed me and yelled at Joan and Marie to hurry up. We all started running for the back door. I did not see my dad anywhere. She threw me in the car, jumped in, and started to drive away fast. As we drove away, the girls and I looked out the back window to see three cars. Parked weirdly in the street at different angles. I could see two guys lying on the ground, bleeding. I thought we were in a race. I have never seen my mom drive so fast before. Both girls and I were asking, "where's Dad?" I wasn't sure if she had lost her hearing or what; all she would say was, "We gotta get home. We were only home long enough to pack me a bag, then dropped me off at my grandpa's. My sister was already with my grandma, so no one had to worry about her, which was something that happened a lot. My sister was always at my grandma's, and it seemed I wasn't wanted there anymore. I dealt with it a lot as a kid for some reason. I wasn't very well-liked. Except for the club and my mom, of course. After my grandpa started having kids with his new wife. It seemed as if he was starting not to like me either. I was running out of family who wanted me around. After being dropped off, I was with my grandpa for a few weeks. My grandpa lived by an intersection with a take-out restaurant on the corner. My grandpa would buy us all food and ice cream every Friday. As much as I enjoyed it, I still wanted my mom to come to get me. I still didn't know who was the one that was bleeding on the couch. I kept seeing the blood on the floor as I wondered why my parents hadn't come to get me. My mom finally came to pick me up; she still wouldn't tell me who had been shot. She said I'll tell you once we get home." I started to cry as I knew it had to be my dad silently. *Why was I crying? I hated my dad for the hurt he caused us.* As I got older, I realized even though I hated him, he was still my father. It took a long time for me to understand why children care so much for the people who hurt them. It's still somewhat of a mystery. Even though my dad hurt me, I still hoped he was not the one on the couch. After getting home, I walked into the house and saw my dad. I was never so happy to see him. I even ran to hug him, thankful he was still alive.

He then took hold of both my arms and said, "Son, Cuddles died. He's gone."

He had been shot three times in the abdomen; he had four different men shooting at him. When the shooting stopped, three were injured, and two were dead. Cuddles, my dad, and Bob had killed two men and wounded two others who jumped into their car and left—leaving one man with half a head and multiple bullet wounds. The other man lay dying from his injuries. At the same time, Cuddles managed to walk into the house and sit on the couch, waiting for the police and ambulance. He was bleeding quite heavily from his wounds. Everyone in the house was screaming and crying. I can only imagine all the screaming and crying was not helping Cuddles at all. Our President lost his battle before reaching the hospital. Life was never the same for so many families, especially mine. After hearing the man I believed could never be killed, was dead all I could do was stand there. I couldn't even cry. *I thought, how?* He was so strong I believed nothing could ever hurt him. It's funny; even now, I can almost see his face. I can picture the look on his face when he ran up to me the day I broke my arm. I went to my room, cried, and just stared at the wall. I wondered, *What are we going to do now? Without him, there's no club. How right I was; my whole life changed from that moment on.* I no longer saw my pals; Shakey and Anus were the only ones I saw. Even at my birthday party, none of the members were there. My dad said we were no longer going to be able to go to the clubhouse anymore. There was a new president, and some members were no longer there. It seemed as if I was losing everyone. My grandparents already wanted my sister to stay with them instead of me. The club was gone. I never felt so alone. I later found out the new President was not only responsible for the shooting of Cuddles. He was also the asshole who wanted to change everything. I personally wondered why he was the new President and not dead. Because no one had the balls to take him on, he got what he wanted. *Personally, I wanted him dead. He took my family away from me.* The club was split up. It was now full of criminals; even Magilla followed him. One night some members shot up our house. We went to my grandpa's house for a few days. After we came back home, I woke up to see Magilla leaving the house. I wanted to see him, but my dad yelled for me to come back. I was upset because he didn't even say hi to me. My dad said he didn't like us anymore. *Later, I found out he had put a gun to my head that morning. Forcing my parents to give up their cuts, broke my heart. This was the guy who threatened to kill someone for putting a toy gun to my head.* I had always thought of this club as being my family. I had no idea what was going to happen from that point on.

CHAPTER 9

My mother's parents were the only grandparents I ever knew. My father's dad died when he was eleven, and he never had a real relationship with his mom. My grandmother, Rose, gave birth to eight children, two from her first husband, whom my father never knew. Then six more from my grandfather, Franklin, whose worst mistake was marrying Rose; not only was she a drunk but a horrible mother. She gave her first two children to their father, which turned out to be the best thing she could have done for them. The following six were not so lucky; the first three were Barb, Beverly, and John, then my father, Berta, and Florie. As Rose lay passed out from being drunk and Franklin was at work. Child Protective Services just walked in the door and took Barb, Beverly, and John. John only survived three days. All three had been wearing a diaper, so long layers of skin came off with the diapers. Barb and Bev suffered terrible infections. After the children were taken, Rose and Franklin were arrested for child neglect, causing death. Once Bev was placed with a family, she later died on the way to the hospital from her appendix bursting, which just left Barb, who was lucky enough to survive. Rose and Franklin were never charged with the death of Bev. *It was her appendix, but truthfully, I believe had it not been for the infections from wearing a diaper so long, I think she would have never died.*

During the first year of being in prison, Rose gave birth to my father, who was taken and placed with his grandparents. Our judicial system was so fucked up they didn't even serve four years. *Honestly, I believe they both should have spent life.* After getting out somehow, they were able to regain custody of my father. Then giving birth to two more children, Berta and Florie. Rose and Franklin returned to their old ways of drinking and doing drugs, which eventually caused my grandfather to have a stroke disabling him from working. Rose decided to start going to bars and bringing strange men home. When my father and two aunts were babies, she would shoot them up to keep them quiet when she brought home strange men. Some were sick child molesters who would molest my father. Some would even physically beat on my grandfather when he would try to get them to leave and turn on my father when he would try to protect his father because this was going on during the forties and early fifties. Things like this were unheard of, which is why so much abuse was unanswered.

Authorities just did not believe this sort of abuse was happening. Many serial killers were getting away with the murders they committed. In such case of Ted Bundy, his murders were during the seventies killing approximately thirty-six women. The women were too trusting, so they easily got into his car. These kinds of murders were unheard of before this time. DNA had not been discovered yet. Otherwise, he would have been caught long before he had the chance to murder so many women. It took him killing and raping a child before they actually did something.

One day while my grandmother was at the bar, my father walked into the bathroom, finding his father lying dead on the floor with his pants down to his knees. He had a massive stroke while using the restroom. My father had to walk to a neighbor's house to use the phone to call the police. *I often wondered what made my father the way he was. I now know.* He would sometimes walk to the bar to try and talk his mother into coming home. As he waited, he would tell the drunk's stories. They would all laugh, patting him on the back and telling him how funny they thought he was. I truly believed he loved the attention these guys showed him, which is why he told so many stories. My father, Berta, and Florie had mental disabilities, which I'm sure was due to the drugs Rose gave them. Florie was worse than Berta. Even as an adult, she had the mind of a child. She would play with stuffed animals and give them names. Berta was my grandfather's second wife. She gave birth to five children, even though my family believes not all five belonged to my grandfather. All five of her children were mentally disabled. *And Florie?* Believe it or not, actually got a real job working in the cafeteria at a major hospital, even living independently. I'm sure the horrible memories of what both of my aunts endured as children haunted them for the rest of their days.

When Berta was around seven years old, she accidentally pulled an old coffee pot down full of scalding water. It gave her fourth-degree burns on her right side, including her upper arm. Since Rose was at the bar, as usual, my father, at twelve-years-old years old, drove all three of them to the nearest hospital. Of course, the hospital was forced to call Child Protective Services due to Berta's burns and the fact a twelve-year-old was the one driving to the hospital instead of a parent. Berta and Florie were put in state hospitals, and my dad bounced from foster home to foster home. Anyone who had to live life in a foster home knows how fun that can be. He had to work on farms and had to endure more abuse.

Not only from the other foster kids but the parents as well. *Who did not teach him any work values* I mean, he didn't mind working. He was not having a boss because he would argue with everyone, which we all know is not a good way to stay employed. As long as he could be his own boss or not have to deal with a boss all the time, he was fine. He would do odd jobs doing mechanics and whatnot. He ended up delivering the Detroit News and Free Press for twenty years or more. It was the only job he could have without dealing with bosses constantly. After my parent's divorce, he met another victim a few years later; having four children with this lady, only two survived—two girls who suffered the same childhood as my sister and me. I tried my best to keep a close eye on them. Hoping he would not hurt them the way he had hurt me. Obviously, again I wasn't able to protect them; breaking my heart, I failed two more sisters. I wasn't told of the abuse until after his death. If I had known he was hurting my little sisters, he would have died much sooner.

CHAPTER 10

When I was around fourteen, I was hanging around with a friend from down the road. His name was Mark, his neighbor had a pool in the backyard. They went camping one summer, so we would sneak down there at night and go swimming. One night my parents were gone. After swimming, we went back to my house and changed clothes. While I was taking off my swim trunks, standing in front of the fan. Mark thought it would be funny to spray pepper spray in the back of the fan. You know where it goes from there, all over my private area. My balls were on fire, and my little man was screaming with burns. Mark was lucky I didn't kill him. It's not easy trying to put your balls in the sink. I wound up having to jump into the tub. He got the hell out of there. I think he knew what was gonna happen when I got out. After calming down, I called him up. I told him, "Dude, you're lucky I didn't kick your ass," as we both were laughing, fuckin prick. After the burning stopped, I couldn't help but laugh. I just wished I could have paid him back by doing the same thing, but he was always watching for it.

Here's something you will learn as you grow up. Children and animals have a sixth sense when it comes to people. They can always sense when there's something odd about someone. I've seen proof of this many times. I've always said if your dog or kid doesn't like someone, don't trust them. When my friend Mark and I delivered newspapers together, there was a corner house where the homeowner wanted us to put the paper in a tube. The problem was they had a damn Cujo chained with a log chain. Every time we tried sliding the paper in, this big ass St. Bernard would come charging. I don't care how thick the chain was; the dog freaked us out. We told them if they wanted their paper in the tube, they would have to move the box or the dog.

One sunny Sunday morning, we were delivering, and of course, my turn to deliver to Cujo. As I walked toward the tube, I noticed the dog was gone. First, I thought, great, he moved the dog. On my way back from sliding the paper into the tube, I heard Mark yelling, "Look Out!" As I looked to where he was pointing, I saw Cujo coming. I froze in time; I couldn't run; all I could do was stand there. I had these thoughts running through my mind. Should I run or maybe act like I was picking something up to throw? It was like everything was moving in slow motion. The dog's lips were going up and down, showing his big ass teeth. I thought for sure I was going to be mauled. When all of a sudden, this dog decided to stop. I know you're not supposed to show fear, but this dog weighed more than I did. As his claws were tearing at the lawn, I couldn't help but shiver and pray. He stopped dead in front of me as I looked down, saying good doggy. He sniffed my pant leg and turned around, and left. I couldn't figure out why the dog did not kill me. The only thing which made sense to me was he sensed I did not pose a threat and could tell I was a good kid. I nearly pissed myself, but I learned to stand my ground lol.

Speaking of dogs, when we lived in my grandma's house in Beecher, where there was no backyard, The neighbor's garage was just outside the front door. They had this ugly mutt chained to the rear corner of the garage facing our house. Every time someone would go outside, this mutt would bark the entire time. He would pull his chain to the end and run back and forth. Slamming his head against the back of the garage, run to the other side and do the same thing WHAM! Slam its head again, all freaking day. This had to be the dumbest animal on the planet, banging its own head all day back and forth. He must have slammed his head one too many times, or they just got tired of having a dumb fucking dog because one day it was gone.

I once built a tree camp with my friends. Good thing I had some building experience. We had to make stilts to extend it out further. Before the stilts, it was barely big enough for two people.

One day a few friends and I were hanging out in the tree camp, and one of them brought a bottle of liquor after stealing it from his grandpa. I had this friend called Tone. He started to drink. At first, a couple of drinks was okay, but then he started sneaking drinks. He got totally drunk. I mean snot flying drunk. Tone and his brother lived with their dad, who didn't take kindly to his son coming home drunk at his age. We tried thinking of a way to sober him up. We tried coffee, any home remedy we could think of, and then I had a thought: *hey, let's get the liquor out of his stomach that should sober him up.* How do we do that? Then I thought of an idea let's make him puke it up. We were coming up blank; one guy said stick your finger down his throat. I thought hell no, he ain't biting my finger; no one else was game for it either. Then I remembered once a club member nearly died from an overdose. Cuddles forced him to drink vinegar; he puked it up and saved his life. I said, "I know; let's make him drink vinegar." I went into the house, grabbed a bottle, and took him into a shed. There I held him down and forced him to drink as much as possible. He puked alright over and over. I started to worry if he was going to puke himself to death. He wound up passing out in a pool of puke, gross. I grabbed a garden hose. Sprayed the shed out and washed him down. It wasn't easy to do, believe me. After the washout, he passed out again. I eventually just told his brother to tell his dad he was staying the night at my house. I was a bit worried his dad would say no, get your ass home. Luckily enough, he didn't. Later, when he woke up, he was still drunk, thanking the kid who had stolen the liquor. Saying it was good. I just wonder if he remembered what he had gone through after getting drunk.

One year when I had just turned fifteen, late in the summer, we were at a beach called Goldenrod. The white folks were jumping from beach to beach due to the blacks moving into the area and basically just taking over the beaches. We used to go to Bluebell Beach. Then it turned into Black bell Beach, which is the way white people preferred to call it. At the time, blacks and whites were at odds worse than today. While at the beach, a park vehicle came driving in fast. Then the next thing we saw was our lifeguard running like a mad dog. We figured someone

50

had drowned. We found out the following morning the person who drowned was Shakey.

Since we were the only family he had, my parents were the ones they called. So we spent the next two days at the hospital. My parents were able to find his father, who had another family, and were able to find his mother, who was in a state hospital. His father told the hospital he didn't even know his son and didn't care whether he lived or died. He signed papers giving my dad rights to do with Shakey as he wanted. The doctors tried to see if they could get a reading from his brain; after a few tries, the conclusion was he was brain dead. My dad had no choice but to take him off life support. One more of my family was gone. After working on getting his mother out for his funeral, she refused to go. *What kind of mother refuses to say goodbye to her only child?* It broke my heart knowing Shakey had no family who cared anything about him. Losing loved ones, one right after another was breaking me down more and more each day.

My parents decided to go and join a carnival right after Cuddles was killed, and believe me when I say that is one of the most complicated ways to live. I mean, now we have cell phones, and almost everyone has one. When my parents worked the carny, there was no cell phone. We had a car for only part of the time. I remember walking down to the restaurant in the morning and taking a cowboy shower, aka) washing in a sink with soap and washcloth. Eating breakfast, walked back, and just basically rode rides all day while my parents worked. As a kid, I had a fuckin blast! My dad worked this thing called a house of mirrors where you have to walk a trail with a shitload of mirrors and try not to bang into them. I personally aced it after a while but had a few knots on my head from wham! Banging my head repeatedly, my mom worked on a game where you try to throw these rings onto pop bottles, and if you can do it, you win a prize. If not, you just keep spending money to keep trying. It was the hardest game I've ever seen. I mean, it was almost impossible. When I was seventeen, I decided to try to work as a carny myself. Living the carny life as an adult fuckin' sucked! Still, no place to sleep unless you have a car or van, and thank God it's summertime!

You can sleep under a ride; hopefully, it doesn't rain. I even sometimes had to sleep in front of a truck. Try pulling the gear shifter out of your ass about eight to ten times a night and showering; fuck that! These guys stood out under a garden hose. The water was so fuckin' cold! I would lose sight of my nuts for at least a week. Starving all fuckin' day trying to get someone's attention to watch your job while you get something. Fuckin' pricks! Like they didn't see me jumping up and down yelling, "HEY ASSHOLE! I'm fucking hungry. "Do you mind?"

I hated that job. I worked as a ride jock only once. It's what they call the guys who work the rides. I worked on the games a couple of times. There was more money to be made, and we would sometimes go in together and rent a room. There was this one guy who I think was Italian. This guy ripped people off. He could talk you out of your gold teeth. He and I worked the same game, and we got along. He gave me a few pointers. He got a hotel every night and invited me to stay, never asking me for any money. He was really cool. I watched him cover his entire bed with cash. If you're going to be a carny, pray you don't get sick because you're fucked! You need to have a van or RV. It's just not a good idea to try it any other way. Not to mention crime, especially nowadays. People are shooting each other left and right, and the government wants to make it nearly impossible for law-abiding citizens to have guns legally. The only people with guns are criminals. I'm sure things are a bit easier with cell phones and actual showers now. I took my kids to a carnival and noticed they had shower trailers. I'm so glad they finally broke down and purchased something to give their people an easier way to keep clean.

CHAPTER 11

One summer, the county was low on funds and wasn't going to be opening the county parks. We all had to find other ways to enjoy nature. One night my cousin Sam, McCall, and I snuck into Stepping Stone Falls Park. We had some beer, a few hooters (aka) joints, or whatever you call them. You wouldn't believe some of the names people have. We were having a blast running around in the dark, drinking, and smoking. We had about as much fun as we could have and were about to leave. As we were walking toward the gate, a park ranger pulled in, showing his lights. We took off as fast as we could toward the trees. McCall was in the front. I figured if there `were anything we were gonna run into, he would hit it first. Sure enough, he tripped over a branch and SPLASH right into a giant mud puddle. I thought, well, better go around. I went around the puddle and waited for McCall to get out of the puddle to lead us into another mess. He did not disappoint. We ran for a minute and ran into a fence that had been there a hundred years or more. As he tried jumping over, he caught his pant leg and ripped a hole in them, cutting his leg. *Believe it or not, he wasn't done there.*

We came up behind the ranger station and hid behind a couple of trees, waiting to make sure the coast was clear to get across the street because we had parked on a dirt side street. Just as we figured it was clear, McCall jumped up and said, "Let's go!" As he started to run, he ran into a low branch. Slamming him on his back and knocking the wind out of him, covering his eye at the same time squealing and rolling around. I tried helping him as soon as he could breathe. He started yelling, "My eye! Oh my freaking god, my eye!"

I told him to quiet down before someone heard him. He started to cry, saying he had poked his eye out. He's asking me repeatedly, "It's gone, isn't it? Oh my fucking God. My eye is gone."

As I moved his hand to look at his eye, it was shut. I told him to open it so I could see. As soon as he opened it, I swear the Niagara Falls poured out. It was really red. I told him his eye was still there. I think he thought I was lying to him because he said, "Are you sure?" I said, "YES! Bro, your eye is still there. It's just fucked up." Needless to say, McCall did not have a good night. My cousin and I came out injury-free.

I have no respect for people who drive drunk. Especially since I had to bury my best friend at nineteen, not to say I myself haven't made an error in judgment and driven under the influence. I did have my limitations and was very unhappy with myself for doing so. I've never been someone who would drink daily only during special occasions. It just isn't my cup of tea.

I still, to this day, miss my friend terribly. He was a great guy, and we had tons of fun. I got a ten-speed for my birthday one year. He and I decided to go riding some back trails. We were moving pretty well and having a blast. All of a sudden, he disappeared into some trees. I thought, where did he go? I found out really quick that as soon as you entered the trees, there was a ditch going straight down then straight up. I never made the up part. I ran right into a log at the bottom, flipped over the handlebars, and just laid there. Until the next thing I knew, I was being stung by a swarm of fuckin' bees. Talk about jumping up and stage left. I was gone with a swarm of bees on my ass. I must have run a mile as fast as my legs could go. I'm not sure how far I ran before they quit stinging me. When I finally got back to where my bike was, Pat was laughing his ass off. I said, "Thanks, Prick. You could have warned me." Then it was about who was going to get the bike. I said, "Hell no! I ain't going down there. 'What if they recognize me?"

He just laughed but ran down there and grabbed it for me. I had to lick my wounds for a few days. He practically lived at my house. We were always doing something crazy. He was even helping my parents and me deliver the Detroit Free Press at night. We had huge routes. One night he decided to steal this bike he had been wanting, and all we could hear was him running down the road with this bike. It had been chained to a metal garbage can. Oh my God, all the banging, he must have woken up half the neighborhood. He lived down the road from my grandma and would go down and shovel the walk so she could walk down to check her mail. My whole family cared a lot about Pat. My dad would tell the story about the bike and garbage can, laugh, and say it was something he would never forget. He disappeared one week, hanging out with these guys, drinking, and driving around. The night of his accident, I saw him telling him he shouldn't be driving around with guys drinking. It was a bad combination, something terrible was bound to happen. Sure enough, that night, they ran out of gas and hitched a ride with some guy who ran a red light at an intersection and ran head-on with another vehicle. His mom said his brain was literally knocked out of his head. He had to have two huge metal plates put in his head. The first time I saw him, I fell to my knees in tears. I didn't even recognize him. I had a tough time talking to him without crying. It was a time when Pittsburgh Pirate hats were really popular, and I happen to have one Pat had been trying to scam from me for months. Before leaving, I told him I was giving him the hat. It was so hard saying goodbye. I cried all the way home. The second time I saw him, he was wearing the hat and smiling. The nurses had told me he would scream if they took the hat off but quiet down as soon as they gave it back. I visited as much as possible. I lived quite a distance from the hospital and did not have a car.

I would have to hitch a ride or walk once he was moved to Frankenmuth. It became almost impossible to visit. His family called me the night he passed and asked me to be a pallbearer. I had to leave the house so my grandma wouldn't hear me crying, Carrying my best friend to his grave was one of the hardest things I ever did until later in the year. I have had to say goodbye to a lot of the friends I'd known as a kid. Nothing scares you more than having people your friends with start passing away, especially when they are close to your age.

I had been living with my grandma for a few years. She had a few scares with her heart but seemed as if it was no longer an issue. Bryan Adams was coming to Detroit, and McCall, along with another good friend, decided to go to the concert, which was on a Sunday. By the time I got home, it was late. Monday morning, as usual, I had to yell out at my grandma because her teapot was whistling away, and she couldn't hear it. I would yell out, "GRANDMA, YOUR COFFEE!"

I suddenly had a strange voice saying, "Get up, go talk to your grandma. It will be the last chance you have to talk to her. I thought, no, I'm tired. I will see her tonight after she gets home from work. The problem was she never made it home. She had a massive heart attack during her lunch break. About the time I knew she would be coming home from work, I asked McCall to drop me off at home. I had been thinking about the voice telling me to get up. I was determined to spend time with my grandma. When we drove by, she wasn't home. At first, I thought how strange she's normally home by now. As we reached the end of the street, my dad pulled up next to us. I could hear my sister crying in the back seat. Immediately, I knew something was wrong, and everything seemed to move slowly. As my mom's friend approached me, she took hold of my arms, saying, "Grandma's gone." I felt as if I was dreaming, wanting to wake up. My heart quit beating. I literally broke to pieces. I cry every time I think about her. A piece of advice: *never ignore that little voice; you will regret it for the rest of your life.* I think everyone, at one time or another, has heard the voice and ignored it. I was nineteen when I lost both my grandma and my best friend. Each loss killed me more and more. It was heart-wrenching.

CHAPTER 12

Within the last nine years, I've lost my club, my best friend, and my grandma. I never felt so alone. I was having to overcome all of this and the horrible memories of my abuse. I contemplated suicide. I thought I had no one, no family, no one to love or love me back. I had been living alone in my grandma's house. I'm emotionally going through a lot at this point. I would sit at the house and just cry myself to sleep. Not even Turner or Allen was there for me. A few months later, I committed myself to a hospital before killing myself; I had to get some help. I was so hurt and broken; I didn't know what I was going to do. After a few weeks of being in the hospital, I met a guy who was hurting as well. After hearing his story, I thought, *wow, seriously, this is your problem? I only wish I had his problems.* I sure as hell wouldn't be there. His situation to me was so minor. I couldn't believe he was there, but I lent my ear and listened to him anyway. I gave him some advice and a shoulder, and we immediately became friends. For some reason, I was able to give him comfort. Which, in turn, gave me something as well; I felt maybe this is why I've gone through so much. Maybe it was to help other people because he felt so much better after telling me his situation and listening to what I had to say. It had given him hope he didn't know he had. We both spent a little over two months at this place. Even once we were no longer in the hospital, we hung out as much as possible. After meeting his family, I wished I could have traded places. He grew up in a nice home with loving parents who I thought were the nicest people. My dad helped me get a job delivering the Free press. I made pretty good money but working a night job was really not for me. I would never make a good vampire. I'm a day person; I would jam the radio as loud as possible. I was doing my best to stay awake, even singing to myself, not to mention no personal life whatsoever, working every night for three hundred sixty-five or sixty-six days. Depending on leap year for the people who want perfection. Either way, you go. Any dating was out of the question unless she was willing to work with you. For sure, it is a dedicated job, and I can't think of any woman willing to go on a date delivering newspapers. I tried working at a small dealership for a short while. But I decided to go back to Flint, living in my grandma's house; it sure sucked living there without her. Everywhere I looked, there were memories of her laughing, joking around, or baking some goodies. Waking up the next morning hoping to hear the coffee pot whistling, I would give anything to yell out one more time. "GRANDMA, YOUR COFFEE!" People truly do not understand how much they love someone until they are gone, and I don't believe they ever will.

After my grandfather passed, it didn't take long for my Aunt Berta to lose everything my grandpa worked for his whole life. It was something he should have known was going to happen. To this day, he still has no headstone on his grave. It is something I could never allow for my wife not to have a headstone, and I'm the only one who has an urn with my father's ashes. I haven't paid to put a stone on my grandfather's grave. Mainly because he dug his own grave now; he has to lie in it. He knew better than to leave her in charge of his affairs, and he left my mom with nothing. She was faithful to him her whole life, and she would have made sure everything was done the way he would have wanted it. My grandmother was guaranteed to have things done her way because she left my mom in charge.

Since the day my grandma sold one of the houses on Tremont. There had been a bunch of people moving in and out. A few years before my grandma passed away, a guy lived there with his girlfriend and daughter. He was a total asshole. On Mother's Day, my grandma and I were getting in the car to visit my mom for the holiday. He came over and told my grandma if she didn't keep her cat in the house, he was going to kill it and put it in her mailbox. I completely freaked out. I told him if he dared touch her cat or ever talked like that to my grandma again, I would kick the living shit out of him. We were about to start fighting when my grandma asked me not to. I told him to get back in his own yard before he got himself seriously fucked up. It took his wife begging him to stop before he decided he better go home. He finally used his head and walked away. *See, just thinking about it gets me pissed off.* There are a lot of things people can get away with, but talking to my grandma like that was not going to be tolerated. I was just looking for any reason to kick his ass, and I got my chance a few weeks later. I took my grandma's branch clippers to the neighbor down the road to have them sharpened. On my way back, I noticed the mailman had just run, so as I walked toward the mailbox, he was doing the same. As we approached the mailbox at the same time, he said something stupid. Now, given that this guy was bigger than I, you'd think he'd be willing to fight fair. Not this pussy. I threw the clippers down to lay into him, and he immediately picked them up to try and cut me with them. I ran up and around his house, cut through his backyard, into my grandma's house, and threw my glasses on the table. I ran out the front door, and we went head up, fighting like dogs. Whenever I'd punch his sissy ass, he'd make me chase him. He ran towards his back door, so I walked over to talk with my grandma because she was getting upset. I thought his pussy ass had quit while talking to my grandma. He ran up behind me as I turned around. He sucker-punched me in the nose. My eyes instantly watered. Luckily enough, I was standing by our back door. I quickly dove inside to catch my wits. Just as I was shaking it off, I could hear my grandma yelling at him.

Worried he might hit her, I ran back out to finish it. He then put his hands up, saying he didn't want to fight anymore. *Too bad I do!* Seeing my grandma so upset, I couldn't upset her even more. The three of us talked it out; he admitted despite my size, I had gotten the better of him. After that, we did our best to stay away from each other. He was still living there after my grandma passed. I did my best to befriend him and his family since we had to live next to one another. The following summer, I threw a party on the fourth of July. I had even invited him and his wife, but he didn't come over. He came over around eleven and told me it was time to send my friends home. *Like who did this motherfucker think he was?* I said,

"Uh, sorry, Dude. What the fuck did you just say? Do you think you're my fuckin' daddy or something?" He said, "My daughter is trying to sleep." "Okay, all you have to do is ask, and we will quiet it down, but for you to tell me I gotta make everyone leave ain't gonna fly." His comeback was that if they didn't leave, he would kick my ass.

Laughing, I said, "Dude, I've already kicked your ass once. you wanna go for round two?" As I lay my glasses on the car, I got blasted with something out of nowhere, and it sure as hell wasn't his fist. I asked, "What did you hit me with? He said," Nothing. My first."

I said, "Bullshit! You ain't man enough to hit me that hard with your fist." Because it was dark, I didn't see it the first time, but I saw it the second. He slipped a piece of garden hose up his sleeve. I said, "You wanna play dirty, motherfucker." I ran into the house and grabbed a bat. By then, he had already run his pussy ass in the house. No matter what I called him or how much I begged him to come back outside, he wouldn't. He knew what would have happened. He had busted my head open. I was bleeding pretty badly. I later found out he had taken a bolt and screwed it at the end of the hose. I wasn't surprised, knowing what kind of coward he was already. I should have known he wasn't man enough to fight fair. This guy wasn't deserving any respect a real man deserves.

I had a few black friends over about a week later. After I told them what had happened, he was standing in the drive. They asked if that was him.

I said, "Yea," and the next thing I knew, they all ran over there and whipped the shit out of him. A few days later, he told a friend if he saw me, he was going to shoot me and did try shooting me a few times. I kept telling him to put his fucking gun down, and we can fight it out. Being the coward he was, he wouldn't do it. One day he yelled out for everyone in my house to get out. Having a shotgun in his hand, he said, "I am coming in to shoot you." He told my sister he wanted to beat me with a baseball bat. She asked, "Why are you such a pussy? You're bigger than he is? You're not man enough to fight?."

That was the way I grew up: fight like a man. If you lose, you lose, but at least you were man enough to stand up for yourself. Not like these pussy asses nowadays.

CHAPTER 13

After moving back to my grandma's house, I partnered with a couple of friends. Making some illegal money, I ran into this kid I had known years ago and hadn't seen in years. His mom used to let him come over and hang out when he was young. My house was as far as she would allow him to go. She apparently liked me then, but that sure changed when we met back up. This kid would come and buy a quarter here and there. One day he pulled into my driveway when I had about three pounds of marijuana on my coffee table, and right behind him was the state police. Everyone in the house freaked out, thinking we were being raided. They were fixing to flush it all down the toilet. Luckily, I stopped them. I said, "Hold on, Brother, if it was a raid, we wouldn't even know they were here until they kicked in the door. *That dumb ass knew what I did; why would anyone be dumb enough to pull into someone's driveway with a cop on his ass knowing what was going on?* I go out there to see what the hell? When the cop told me, he was already pulling him over when he pulled into my drive. I told the cop, it was not a problem, and I was just wondering." *Why did he choose my drive? Of course, this dumb fuck doesn't have legal plates; he didn't even have a driver's license.* His mom thought I should have argued with the cop. Saying I wouldn't allow him to tow the car. I didn't give a shit what he did with that car. I'm not arguing with no cop. His momma was mad at me. *Ask me if I give a shit. NOPE!* Before I was banned from my friend's momma's house, there were a couple of brothers who were always there. Ricardo and Roberto, Ric had a crush on Dean's sister, who in turn had one on me. So we would sit in the basement where everyone hung out. I would make out with the sister, which Ric did not like at all. *Ask me if I gave a shit. NOPE!* That was me at that time. I didn't give a shit about anything. The lady across the street from me said I was an asshole. I said, "Yup, been an asshole for twenty years, will be an asshole for another twenty."

Around the time my parents were getting a divorce, *about time, I thought. I'll never understand why she didn't do that when I was a kid.* It turned out that while working at a state hospital, she developed a friendship with one of her students. After the student was no longer in the hospital, my mom stayed in touch. One day my mom drove and picked up the student, who turned out to be female. I became romantically interested in this girl. My mom kept saying you don't want to try to be in a relationship. I couldn't figure out what she had against us being together. It didn't take long for me to figure out why. It turned out the two of them were having a relationship. Imagine my surprise. I never figured I would have competition with my mom over a chic. As I'm sure you can imagine, that did not go very well. I was already disgusted she was messing around with a teenage student but a female too. I wasn't sure who I was more disgusted with, my mom or the girl. Things were a bit difficult between my mom and me after that. It wasn't something the family was willing to accept. Especially since I was involved, I was angry at the deception of thinking I was in this relationship.

When in fact, she was cheating on me with my mother! I wanted her to wise up and leave my father, but not like this. While this whole thing with my mom and her student was going on. I lived upstairs in a rented room. I got a job at a dry-cleaning company called One Hour Martinizing and was driving a 1972 Nova; the damn thing barely had any heat. One morning I was running a bit late, and it was nearly twenty below zero and not counting the wind chill. They warned folks to bring in the animals so they wouldn't freeze to death. I ran out of gas right in front of Bloomfield Hills High School.

I knew I would freeze to death trying to walk to a gas station. Plus, my car was in the left lane. I didn't want to leave it; cops would most likely tow it. I thought maybe I could give it a quick push. Coast down this steep ass hill as far as it would go, and maybe I could get in the right lane and be much closer to a gas station. I would have to take my chances from there. I rolled my window down, got out, and shut the door. Being in the left lane with all the traffic, someone coming would surely hit my door, killing me. As I got it rolling, I opened the door quickly to get in. As I started to get in, the car swerved towards the oncoming traffic, so as quickly as I could, I shut the door and reached in to grab the steering wheel to bring it back into my lane. This is where the protective instinct nearly killed me. I was steering the car from the outside the car got going too fast. I wasn't able to get in or stop it. The only thing going through my mind was I'm not letting this car go to kill some innocent person. I wasn't willing to let someone die because of my stupidity. As the car went faster, the faster I ran. I can't tell you how fast my legs were going. I just know I had never run as fast in my life. By the time I reached the bottom, I was pulling so hard on the steering wheel and mirror. I bent the steering wheel and broke my mirror. Needless to say, I was no longer cold. In fact, I was sweating so bad my hair was dripping, and the next thing you're not going to believe, a cop with his lights on pulled in behind me. I thought for sure I was going to jail, and actually, I wasn't upset about it. I figured at least his car had heat; as I held my hands up, walking toward the officer, he put his hand out to shake my hand. A bit confused, I reached out and shook his hand; he said," You have got to be either the bravest or craziest man I've ever seen. Do you know where I was parked?" I replied, "Uh, no."

He pointed up the hill across the school; he watched the whole thing. His only regret was that he didn't have a video camera because he could have won home's funniest videos. He was grateful I didn't let the car go. It would have definitely killed someone. He also pushed my car to the gas station. As I was thanking him, he asked, "Do you, by chance, have your driver's license on you?" Knowing not only did I not possess a driver's license, but the plates on my car were illegal. I said, "Sorry, I was running really late and forgot my wallet." He just said, "Okay, listen, I knocked your plate off, pushing you. I will bring your plate up to your job." As I was working, I was worried he would come and arrest me. As soon as he ran my plate, he would see it didn't even belong to my car. Right after lunch, I was working in the back. I heard the door open, and there he was. I started shaking, thinking he was going to ask to speak with me. Instead, he handed over my plate and said, "Please give this to Mr. Taylor."

I felt God was shining down on me. WHEW.

While living in my grandma's place on Tremont. One day, an old friend came and stayed with me for a short time with her boyfriend. She was friends with a girl from down the road. Little did I know she was to be my first wife. We were together for almost a year. When her stepmom told us to either get married or quit seeing each other. I thought how strange, here she hates me, and to get rid of me is to sign papers allowing me to marry her. Isn't that going to cause us to see each other that much more? Not that I liked her any better. I can't describe a woman like this. Jean was sixteen when we got married. It was wrong to force a sixteen-year-old to marry someone to keep the relationship. Let's just say neither mother-in-law, nor I liked each other at all. She never smiled, and her biological daughter was the same way, ugh, but I liked the dad. He was a good, hardworking guy. *Why would he marry that old battle ax? I'll never understand.* Our wedding was one of those let's go cheap weddings. It turned out better than I thought. Her parents sure weren't going to help us with it, and I was far from rich. With my family and friends, we made it pretty good. I had Allen as my best man and my friend from the hospital as my second. Turner didn't even show. I was truly hurt he wouldn't even come to his best friend's wedding. We tried to put a sign on our front door saying just married. You would normally think, hey, they just got married; let's give them some privacy. Hell no! These bastards still banged on our door. They didn't give a shit; they just wanted their weed.

CHAPTER 14

Our first pet was a tiny little runt. My dad and his new wife lived across the street from Allen and his girlfriend. Since Allen was my best friend and my partner Jean and I was at his house quite often. I saw my dad outside, so I went over to chat; he was trying to feed his dog, whom he had locked in a van because she just had pups. The dog kept trying to bite him; he told me she wouldn't let anyone near her. I looked and noticed she didn't have any water. I said, "Well, she's dying of thirst; she needs water. I went and got her dish and filled it. He said," She didn't have any because he or his wife couldn't get near her. Not without her trying to bite them." I'm thinking, *what did he do to this dog to make her hate them?* I gave her a bowl of water. She only wanted me to give her attention. I stood there while he gave her some food, petting her and giving her attention. She was just a big baby to me, not even a growl. Then one day, I came to Allen's to find my dad had moved out. I was shocked he didn't even say anything about moving. The worse thing is he left the fuckin' dog in the van with her pups. To say the least, I was pretty pissed off. *Why would he abandon them?* I went over to make sure she had food and water. There was a bag of food lying all over the floor but barely any water, so I gave her some. While still at Allen's, I had a few drinks. We heard the dog attacking the puppies. It was horrible. I thought I was going to find dead pups.

Luckily, not dead, but I found one bleeding from his face and shaking like a leaf. I couldn't leave this little guy to be killed. We adopted him and took him home. He looked like a little bitty bear cub. We just named him Bear that summer; we barely had any rain; it was so freaking hot. We didn't even have any grass in our yard. We tried staying inside even though there was no air conditioning, and people think they have it rough now. Try living in a house or driving a car with no air.

Bear grew up bigger than I thought he would. I used to take him to the beach; he loved fetching in the water. I was once at Goldenrod Beach, and Bear was running in for his stick. One time he couldn't find his stick, so instead of coming back empty. He grabbed hold of the rope tied to the buoy. Determined to bring it in, he was pulling it pretty hard. You would have thought they saw Jaws. People ran out of the water screaming. *I had no idea why It was. a dog, not a crocodile.* At my grandpa's family reunion, one of my grandpa's kids wanted to hold the leash and walk him. I told him to hold on tight and don't let go. He's pretty strong. We got by the water, and I quietly told my other cousin to throw a stick. Standing on a small hill, my cousin was walking Bear, who was clueless about what was about to happen. Larry threw the stick, and you would have thought my dog got struck by lightning. He took off so fast he jerked poor John off his feet, nearly dislocating his shoulder. Bear dragged him across the beach. Larry and I kept yelling, "LET GO!"

John couldn't get his hand free until Bear went into the water. After noticing he was okay, just a few scrapes and wet. We were laughing so hard that I was getting cramps. The look on his face was priceless. Luckily, John was a good sport about it. I don't remember what ever happened to that dog which bothers me because I loved Bear; he was my pal. In the summer of 1989, my dad had given my new wife and me a van as a wedding gift. It was the van my dad had Bear's mother in, but hey, it was a vehicle we didn't have; the only bad thing was that no one could drive it but me since it was a three-speed stick on the column. It was called three on a tree. We decided to take my stepsister, Nan, and her boyfriend to a place to swim, with a rope tied to a branch overlooking the water. We were having a great time. We cooked a little food and had a few drinks. We were swinging out, coming back for a good swing out, and jumping in the water. I swung back and forth one too many times, and when I swung back in, I swung a little too far to the right, and there was another tree. I could see myself about to slam into it. I quickly thought, *OH NO! What am I going to do?* At first, I thought maybe I should let go, but I figured it would hurt worse. So I toughed it out, fuck that tree, I thought, WHAM! I slammed into it. Immediately I started to spin. As soon as I saw the water, I let go. I don't remember much after that. As I was coming to, I could hear voices, as I saw myself coming out of the water. I saw Jeff coming toward me, calling my name. He said, "You were underwater for almost five minutes."

Needless to say, I was ready to go home. My right arm was skinned up so bad I could barely move it. Oops, we have another problem. I'm the only one who knows how to drive this damn thing. Jeff said he'd driven a stick before but never like this one. My wife didn't even know how to drive. It looked like I had to figure something out. I figured I would have to talk Jeff through it as I sat in the passenger seat trying to coach him. Listening to the grinding of my gears, I started to think maybe he had lied about ever driving a stick. I was thinking of the old saying if you can't find 'em grind them. I told him to pull over. While driving, I coached him on shifting for me as I couldn't move my right arm. We made it without an accident or getting pulled over, thank God. For most of my life, I owned cars with no air conditioning. I often wonder how in the hell did we survive without it.

Not long after I was married, Jean's best friend's dad started coming over and hanging out. He and I were friends from the start. He was just a year or two older than my mom, and I thought, hey, let's introduce them. About a year and a half later, my mom and Glenn got married. They were married by the same reverend as my wife and I. The family, my grandma's family, was friends with. He and his wife were my Cub Scout leaders. I had known them my whole life; at first, it was cool to have my mom back with a man, especially since she married a friend. It wasn't long after his two youngest became a serious pain in the ass. The boy couldn't keep his hands off other people's belongings. He kept taking my mom's stuff which belonged to my grandma. He's lucky I didn't kill him over it, plus Glenn was drinking a bit to much and wouldn't listen to anyone but me. I kept having to go over there and referee. Trying to calm him, this went on for about the first year. Before he realized he had to quit before he wound up single again. I think people should know when they have a problem with drinking;

they become someone no one likes. Maybe it should not be your drug of choice, or they should know when to say when. Glenn's two youngest turned out to be a real issue. With the boy not keeping his hands off things and the girl was just being defiant. As they got older, it got worse. The boy was breaking into the house stealing, and the girl was dating nasty homies. My mom and husband had to put bars on the windows and doors to keep the boy out. The girl was skipping school constantly. She eventually just quit and moved in with her cousin, who was having babies from black men. She decided that was her future as well. Eventually, she got hooked on drugs and lost custody of all three of her kids.

CHAPTER 15

In the summer of 1988, Allen was telling me our other partner got a job at the Palace of Auburn Hills. He thought we should also try to get a job there, so we headed down there, met up with our friends, and got hired. The Palace had about six of our neighborhood friends working with us. I went to school with most of them talk about fun. We had a blast the first year setting up the concerts. We knew all the Pistons. All the bad boys from the 1988 Detroit Pistons were there. John Salley, Darrell Dawkins, Isaiah Thomas, and the whole crew. Eight pals were setting up tearing down all those concerts and the basketball floor. Allen and I really enjoyed it. It was one fun year. The following year my dumb ass turned down the job of a lifetime. It just so happened Madonna was playing the Palace, and I was lucky enough to work in production. I worked with the crew setting up the stage. Have you ever met someone, and it seemed as if you'd known them for years? The Stage Manager for Madonna was that someone. He and I were friends from the start. The two of us were joking back and forth. He started to tell me how to set up a part of the stage I had done before. Jokingly, I said, "Don't worry about me, Bro; I got this." He said, "oh, so you think you know how to do this, huh?" As he started hollering, "Hey, everyone, stop working for a sec; I've got an announcement, Taylor's in charge, so if you have any questions, ask him." At that time, there were five guys with the same first name. So everyone got called by their last name except one because his was Rose. Ain't no guy wants to be called Rose. I said, "Whoa, bro, hold on a sec; I didn't say I knew the whole thing." He said, "Don't worry about it; if they ask you something and you don't know, just give it your best; if you need my help, I'll help you." I thought, what the hell, why not so? I gave it the best I had. I was nearly in charge of that whole stage with only a few questions. Throughout the day, as we were working, he had been telling us he would no longer be in charge of the stage. Madonna was leaving the country and didn't want to go that far away from his family. He was done after the next stop, and as far as he knew, they did not have a replacement. After everything was done, he asked me, "If I were to show you one more time how to set up the stage, Do you think you would be able to set it up by yourself?" I told him, "maybe, but I can't say for sure."

He said, "I believe you could and if I wanted, "I would recommend you and almost guarantee the job." My jaw nearly hit the floor. I couldn't believe he had faith in me. It made me feel proud this guy had a hard job. Those stages are no joke, and for him to see my talent in the one day, we worked together. It made me feel pretty good. I told him I had to talk to my wife and think about it. Of course, the wife was saying I would probably wind up sleeping with Madonna. I mean, seriously, like all the guys she had to choose from, she'd pick me. I told her not to be ridiculous, but she was right about one thing. It would be hard not to cheat with all the women I would be meeting. I still kick myself because it would have made my life so different. My marriage didn't last anyway. I wound up getting Ricardo and my wife a job there at the Palace. Ric worked on my crew, and the wife did housekeeping. Ric was this really short guy who was almost completely bald at thirteen. I always teased him saying. It was because he once came close to losing three of his toes after messing around with a manhole cover. Someone thought they saw a cop and dropped it, and he was standing a bit too close, and WHAM! Down on his toes, it went. Luckily enough, he kept them. The two and half years I spent working at the Palace was one of the best jobs I ever had. We helped put up the WWF wrestling ring more than once; the second time, we had to bring the ring all the way around through the concert room because we had already set up Aerosmith, who had a concert the day before, and another one the following day. Too big a job to take it down just to put it back up again. It was so cool being a part of it. Once we were done, Ric and I jumped in the ring, running up against the ropes. We wound them so tight they truly threw you forward. After we were done playing. We had to get back to work, so Ric went off to do one job, and I went to do another. As I was walking from the ring, we put up a curtain so the wrestlers wouldn't be seen until their music started. As I walked, I saw these huge legs under the curtain. I came in and saw the biggest man I'd ever seen. I mean, this guy was a monster with arms bigger than my head. The man turned out to be the Warlord from Powers of Pain. He looked down at me, and I looked up. He asked, "WHAT'S UP?" Damn, he was big; we just started chatting. He was such a cool guy. He didn't talk any differently to me than he would anyone else. He's a real down-to-earth kind of person. We walked down the hall to where a bunch of wrestlers were standing around talking. The next thing I knew, Virgil, Ted DiBiase's so-called bodyguard, started acting like he wanted to box with the Warlord. I asked, "Virgil if he was crazy? This guy could kill you, Dude." Just as this was going on, Ric happened to be walking toward me. The Warlord swooped his huge arm at Virgil. Ric had stepped behind Virgil and slammed Ric against the wall. Ric hollered, "Hey! MAN! Watch what you're doing!" This is a big man slamming into such a little guy. I even got to meet one of the largest men in the world, Andre, the Giant, who told me a story about him being arrested in Iowa because of a paparazzi photographer who kept taking pictures. He asked the guy to quit, and the guy ignored him. After the next picture he took, Andre grabbed him by his jacket, then his ankle flipped him upside down, and shook him till his pockets were empty. The police were forced to use shackles for the legs to handcuff his wrists because his wrists were too big for regular handcuffs.

My favorite wrestler by far was Brutus the Barber Beefcake. He was such a friendly, good-hearted guy. Turner's little boy was his biggest fan, so I took him to the matches and brought him down to meet Brutus. You would have thought his little eyes were going to fall out. They got so big Brutus took the T-shirt he bought and put a huge autograph. That little boy treasures that shirt even to this day.

The job brought something different every day. The New Kids on the Block came into town. The morning the tickets went on sale. It was around January and cold as shit. We had to go and set up bike racks so that we could let all these mothers in who wanted to buy tickets for their little princesses. They had camped out in front of the doors OVERNIGHT! I mean, *what is wrong with these people?* Sleeping outside in the winter just to buy tickets. They were acting like children fighting as to who was there first. We had to get these women in a line to keep them from killing each other. I just couldn't believe these full-grown people acting like that. Come concert day, we set up the stage and chairs and then changed most of the men's restrooms into women's because there were so many girls. I felt like a fat man in a candy store. I saw the most beautiful woman I had ever seen in my life. None of the guys could pick what girl they would rather have, the one standing to the left or the one on the right.

The Palace even had some gymnastics events watching these kids jump around doing flips. It was definitely cool, especially since we were only like twenty feet from it. I watched from the area where the gymnasts exited the arena after they were done. There was this young gymnast about twelve years old standing beside me. She said she was waiting for her friend to get done. This little girl's name was Amy. I remember it so well because this full-grown woman kept screaming her name with her arms out, yelling, "Amy! Amy! My little angel Amy! I love you." I thought to myself, *is this woman obsessed with a little kid?* The little girl was so scared she grabbed my arm. I told her, "Don't worry, I won't let anyone touch you." I mean, wow, people are freaking nuts! I couldn't believe it might be possible for me to have to fight this woman off this kid.

We had this guy who was our crew leader. We called him Brown Nose Pat because whenever there was some bullshit job, he would jump on the radio saying my guys will do it. One day we got a bit pissed off and told him to quit referring to us as his guys. Before you volunteer us for some bullshit work, ask us. What an asshole! No one liked him. Not only did he have a brown nose he also had two different colored eyes. I started making Steve Austin's bionic sound as he counted salt bags. I told him, "Just use your bionic eye, Pat."

All of us got along well with a few of the Detroit Pistons. One, in particular, Rick Mahorn, we were always teasing back and forth. One day after practice, he was leaving the arena, so we started whispering, "Hey, let's jump his big ass when he gets around the corner. He overheard us. He said, "Y'all gonna do what?" We said, "We are going to jump your big ass." He asked, "For what?," "We want your jersey." He said, "Ya ain't gotta jump me. Here take it." He actually took it off and gave it to us. I mean, what a cool guy. Of course, we were joking about jumping him. It was the kind of guy he was. We sure missed him when they traded him just didn't seem the same without him. John Salley was my favorite. He was always trying to bet me twenty dollars he could make free throws with his eyes closed. I kept trying to stomp on the floor so he would miss. Whenever he saw me, he'd yell, "What's up? Taylor?"

.The Pistons won the championship the first year, so the suits upstairs wanted us to build a stage in the center of the arena. When the players' received their rings, they could say something to the fans. Fans were allowed free entrance into the Palace for the ceremony. They wanted the stage a specific size, and no one could figure out how to do it. The supervisor said, "We just don't have the parts." I told them:" Yes, we do." We argued for a few minutes because they didn't think I knew what I was talking about. Finally, they agreed to listen. By this time, I was a bit angry because they would never listen to any of my suggestions until I proved it to them. With somewhat of an attitude, I started putting things together, and ten minutes later, BAM! DONE. I figured maybe they might listen to me now.

My father always thought I was stupid, which pissed me off. I'm a lot smarter than people gave me credit for. After we finished putting up the stage, we had to start cleaning under the risers, which are the chairs we laid down and pushed in or pulled out. When they opened the doors under, it sounded like elephants coming down, nearly blowing our ears out.

The suits upstairs, thinking they were so smart, came up with the plan to refinish the basketball floor. It was a good idea, but they forgot to inform the night crew to disassemble the floor because the basketball floor was three hundred pieces of a jigsaw puzzle. The day they were doing it, we were coming out of the concert room when I noticed they were brushing fresh varnish on the floor while it was still put together. The first thing I said was, "Hey, what are they doing? You better stop them. It is going to super glue the floor together." Sanders, the supervisor, said, "Don't worry, they know what they're doing. It's a special kind of varnish." I said, "Really? What kind is that?" I don't care how special it is; there's no way It's gonna work out.

Then again, don't listen to me, you'll see. Sure enough, a week later, the night crew was supposed to pick the floor up and put up the boxing ring. As I predicted, the floor wasn't even half done. They were chipping at the seams with screwdrivers. I looked at Sanders and said, "Special varnish, huh+?" He told me to shut up; he didn't want to hear it. But he knew I wasn't shutting up. I went on all day about it. I wound up trying to fix the floor with staples and glue. The last piece that got laid down would never lock. *How did they not know the floor was a big puzzle?* We were even on television taking the floor up right after they won the championship. Dummies! They should have had the common sense to ask.

I was the main fork truck driver. I was good at it. I even carried basketball hoops around the hallway, which was a circle because the building was round. The following summer, some dumb-ass kid was driving around the parking lot, putting the fork truck in neutral as he was going down a hill to pick up speed. He had his forks down too low, and they hit the concrete flipping the fork truck right on top of him, killing him instantly. From then on, anyone driving a fork had to take a test to prove they could drive it safely. I had no problem taking it; the test was easy. I had been driving one for a while now.

A few months after passing the test, Brown Nose Pat said, "I can't drive anymore because you didn't have a driver's license." I said, "Dude, I'm not driving it around town; this is private property." He was just being an asshole; we hadn't gotten along since the shoveling day. We had gotten a few new people because some of my school chums had quit. One of the guys was a bit older than I, and they were giving a few promotions to supervisors. Well, Brown Nose Pat was definitely one who got one of them. The second promotion was going to be for one of us. I thought for sure it would be me. I had more seniority than anyone, plus I knew the place inside out. There was nothing I didn't know how to do. This was going on just after the Pistons won their second championship. Charles Barkley had been hanging out in our office to avoid the media; again, he and I hit it off. When Pat was an asshole to me, Barkley told him, "Don't mess with my boy, Taylor." Which is what everyone called me. He also told me, "If you ever need a job, let me know. I will make sure you have one." Because I believed I would get the supervisor's job, so I told him, "I was happy here." When it came time for my promotion, I got the news the new guy Mike got the job. Talk about hurt. I was not only hurt but also humiliated. I had been there for over two years. I knew the job inside out. I deserved it. For them to spit in my face really bothered me. After talking with Joan Jett a few days later, I no longer cared for my job. I asked her if she would autograph our office door. It was something we did as a crew. We would get celebrity autographs on the inside of our office door.

As we were walking toward the office, fat ass Pat came running around the corner waving his arms and yelling, "JOAN, JOAN!" She immediately jumped behind me, thinking he was a crazy fan. I told her not to worry. It was just my fat-ass boss embarrassing me, and then he pretended I wasn't even there. Not only did he scare the shit out of her, but he pissed me right off. Even made her give me the evil eye when she came out. I didn't feel at home there anymore. I felt like I had been stabbed in the back. The people who worked there were getting worse and worse. We were setting up Janet Jackson. I was laying down chairs, and there was this girl from housekeeping who kept throwing our sodas in the garbage. I just bought one, took a few drinks out of it, and went back to laying chairs, came back for another drink, and the bitch had thrown it away. I bought another and saw her on my way back. I asked her, "Did you throw my soda away?" She said, "I did, and if you sit that one down, I will throw it away too." By now, I was seriously pissed off. I cracked it open, took a drink, and sat it down. I told her," If you dare to touch it, I will break her fuckin' fingers." She went crying to her boss, telling him I threatened to break her fingers. He asked me, "Did you tell her you would break her fingers?" I said, "Yes, sir," and explained the situation, not that I would ever harm her. I was just angry at the moment. That was all Pat needed. He had a good reason to get rid of me; in one way, I was glad, but in another, I was upset. I busted my ass to do a good job there, and how do they repay me? They spit in my fuckin' face. It hurt me deeply. I truly loved my job; the guy didn't know anything but what I taught him about the job; as far as I was concerned, I had been seriously cheated.

CHAPTER 16

In August 1990, Iraq invaded Kuwait to gain more control over the oil supply. The US demanded Saddam Hussein withdraw his troops which he refused to do. Operation Desert Shield began. Then a few months later, it turned into Operation Desert Storm. Then it changed to a different name. The Persian Gulf War, no matter what they called it next. It was the same fuckin' war. We didn't pull out of Iraq until 2021. So for thirty-one years, this ignorant ass war continued, and the bad part was the terrorists won anyway. Please don't ask me how a country not even the size of Texas can beat thirty-five nations.

Personally, I would have blown the hell out of it. They wanted to go over there, pussyfooting around, and we lost a lot of good soldiers. Not just from the US but in other countries as well. Not to mention we left a shit load of helicopters and tanks and God knows what else. In 1991 Bill Clinton became our President. He blew some shit up over there, but then we started to fix all the shit we blew up, like seriously!! I wouldn't have fixed shit. I would have blown up more shit and more until every last Al Qaeda was dead, Taliban, or whatever they want to call themselves. *I just can't believe it went so long; we should have won that war years ago. We went through six presidents with that shitty ass war.* I personally didn't feel ole Bill was a bad president. He was the only one besides Andrew Jackson who left office without a deficit. Not to mention

I had work climbing out of my ears. The only thing ole Bill had a problem with was women; he had a problem keeping it in his pants. He even had a cutie pie blowing him in the oval office, which was his personal business, but he kept getting caught. What was weird was Hillary didn't leave him. Not like she needed his money; she was born with a silver spoon in her mouth. I honestly believe she was just a freak. She was probably standing there in the oval office wearing a cheerleading outfit with some pom poms yelling, "GO BILL! GO BILL!"

I had been mistreated my whole life and was fed up with people disregarding me like I didn't matter. It made me wonder what I could have done to deserve all of this. Getting my wife a job there was a mistake as well. As soon as I no longer worked there, she started messing around with a coworker. What was really bad was she waited to cheat after we had our first child. I was never so happy at the thought of being a father. I swore to be the father I never had. I would never hear the words I hate you from my child. I did, however, hear those words being said by my wife, which literally broke my heart. Living the violence, I had seen with my own eyes watching my father hit on my Mom. I started to become the man I hated. I had no idea how to be a husband, and she had no idea how to be a wife. We were kids; her parents had set us up for failure from the get-go. We weren't ready to get married; we just wanted to be together. For them to force us to marry or break up was wrong. The only good thing coming out of it was our daughter. I had never truly known what love was until I held my baby. She was my world. It wasn't long after our daughter was born that I found out about the affair with her coworker. It's when she said the words I had hoped I would never hear. Had I known which guy it was, he would have found himself on the other side of my shoe. I would have beaten him bloody after all I had been through. I would have no problem beating the living shit out of him. I finally had a family, and for him to take my family from me, I was completely devastated. To hear her say she hated me and was seeing someone else drove me just to take off and go on a drinking frenzy. I went walking around drinking Mad Dog. I drank myself crazy.

I can remember waking up to my wife coming into the house; after that, I only remember bits and pieces. Finding out the next morning what I had actually done drove me to put a gun in my mouth. This wasn't the first time I've tried killing myself. When I was sixteen, I took a bottle of my dad's emphysema meds. My Mom noticed I was sick later and could not get a temperature reading and took me to the hospital. They forced a tube up my nose and into my stomach to pump out the drugs. Had I not gotten to the hospital when I did, I would have surely died. The gun I was going to use was a sixteen-gauge sawed-off shotgun.

I pulled the trigger. Luckily, I forgot to put a bullet in. I put one in but just before, I started to pull the trigger the second time. I heard a voice saying, "I hate you, Daddy; Why would you leave me? Did you not love me?" I'll never forgive you.." The thought of my daughter saying she hates me broke me. After I swore, she would never say those words. It made me stop and just cry as I emptied my bottle of liquor. I sold the gun a few days later, and never even to this day have I bought another gun. From then on, I have never drunk a bottle of wine, even to this day. All I wanted to do was get my family back. My wife took my daughter and disappeared. I was scared I was never going to see them again. I did find out my wife was still working at the Palace. I tried reaching her but had no luck. When I did find out where they were. I asked my Mom and sister if they would go talk with her. After a few months, I started to spend more time with my daughter, but my marriage was over.

I told my wife to take our daughter home, and I would be the one to leave. It didn't last long. When I came to get my daughter because I was keeping her while Jean worked the night shift, she told me I couldn't have her. I knew something was wrong, so I forced my way in and found the baby with a huge scab on her nose. With no good reason as to how she got burned on her nose. It looked as if someone had put a cigarette on her nose. I then decided to get a divorce and get full custody. While in court over our divorce, she was already seven months pregnant, and the judge did not take that lightly. She basically said he called her a whore. I had no sympathy. I said, "If the shoe fits.."

CHAPTER 17

In March 1992, a friend asked if I wanted to help him start a business doing roofing. I had saved up some money by selling my green and working the third shift at the plastics factory. When one night, some guys kicked in my front door claiming to be cops and stole some money and green while I was at work. Of course, that shit would have never happened had I been home. Someone would have been stabbed, and I would have had no problem killing anyone kicking in my door. They even busted my pregnant girlfriend in the head with the butt of a pistol. What piece of shit hits a woman, especially one who's pregnant?" I quit the night job. I really didn't need the money anyway. I was making enough on my own. I thought the offer over and figured why not. It's a way of learning a trade and making some money doing it. It took a little time, but I eventually got it down. Obviously, not quick enough for Larry because just as soon as we were making decent money, he decided to go his own way. He was leaving me in a bit of a situation. I still needed some help to improve. A bit of advice: *people only care about themselves and what you can give them.* Luckily, I was able to purchase a good set of tools. We bought our materials from James Lumber from a guy named John. We spent so much money there that John let me take a brand-new nail gun and pay him for it the following morning. I was there the next morning with the money thanking him for trusting me. I never had anyone trust me with something like that before. I'm talking about over three hundred dollars worth, and Larry left me at lousy timing. I had two jobs going and didn't know much about flashing walls. He even took the business name I had put so much money into. Right around then, my girl gave birth to my second daughter, Lynn. Even though a few friends thought I should quit, I couldn't. I wasn't the type to just give up, so I kept working. I was determined. I pushed forward until I was one of the best roofers in town. Even the Mayor of Flint said he had heard of my company. I used to do some work with this family. Their last name was Dick. They were some smart guys. All three were builders, so I got to learn how to do a bit of framing, and they gave me all the roofing work. We were building this house around March, so it was cold some days but not freezing. I had one guy with me laying the plywood for the roof. It was a decent day, so Chris and I were slamming them down. We finished one side and were about to go around the back. I was about to start lowering my air gun down the back, but some guys were working back there, and I didn't want to hit anyone. I went to bring my knee up to look over the top, and soon as I did, I heard the air gun go off, startling me, and you'll never guess what I fuckin did. I put a two-and-a-half-inch staple through my knee cap. Damn IT! I immediately tried to get my fingers on it to pull it out. It was too deep, so I hollered for someone to hurry and get me a pair of pliers. The builder says, "What in the hell do you need pliers for?" I told him what I had done, and so he freaked out, yelling, "Don't you fuckin' dare touch it. Get down here!" Chris came running over, and I couldn't straighten my leg out. It was stapled in a bent position, and it wasn't moving. I told Chris to set me on the plywood and bring me down with the Skytrax. He lifted me onto the plywood, and Brent brought me down. I'd never seen anyone act like that before! over something so minor; there wasn't even any blood. I kept telling him just to give me some pliers, and I would pull it out and go back to work.

He said, "No, you ain't. Don't you touch it." He kept pacing back and forth, talking to himself, saying, "Oh my God! Oh my God!" I said, "Brent, it's just a staple, man. Chris went and cut his damn fingers off with a saw now that was bad." He kept trying to talk me into getting in the van and going to the hospital. I can't straighten my leg. My leg was stapled into a V. These guys picked up the plywood I was on, slid me in the back of the pickup truck, and drove me to the hospital. Thank God it wasn't cold out. The problem was Chris, and I had been cutting plywood all morning. The sheet I was on was covered with sawdust; the sawdust didn't blow out of the truck; that shit blew like a hurricane. I had it in my mouth, ears, eyes; you name it; I was even shaking it out of my hair. It was the longest fuckin' ride of my life. Boy, oh boy, good times.

About six months after my second daughter was born, I couldn't take it anymore. Her Mom was so jealous of everything, even my three-year-old. I had to get away from her. I made her move out, and she would always drive by my house. McCall and his girlfriend were over one night, and Marie stopped with my daughter, saying the baby wants to see you.

I said, "She's barely six months old. I don't think she asked you, hey, let us stop by dads." I told her, "I would like to visit with her as long as you don't start fighting with me. I won't put up with it; you'll have to leave." She said she wouldn't, so I put Lynn in her walker and started to play with her, and not even ten minutes later, Marie started wanting to argue. I listened to her for a few minutes but finally said, "You gotta go; I'm not gonna be arguing." The next thing I knew, she jumped up and grabbed Lynn by her arm and tried jerking her out of the walker; the walker was still attached. I tried taking the baby from her before Lynn got hurt. Marie would not let go; she had the baby in a death grip. It took all three of us to get the baby away. Lynn could literally not breathe. I was so mad I told Marie to leave, and I wasn't giving her my daughter. She called the cops, and after explaining what happened to the cop, he agreed not to give her back. I said the only person I would release her to was Marie's aunt. I was still friends with her and trusted her not to let Marie hurt my little girl.

I wound up moving back into my grandma's place. I moved to the east side of Flint for over a year. I was renting out my grandma's place, which did not work out. I moved because my grandma's place was really small, and having two kids, I thought we needed more room, but after the split with Marie. It was just Koler and me again. It was the home I knew the most anyway, and it felt odd having someone else living there. Marie was so obsessed she moved into the house next door to me, which did not make my personal life very easy. It felt like I had eyes on me constantly. Her boyfriend, Jimmy, was with her when she moved in. It didn't matter; Whenever I had a lady over, Marie constantly asked, "Who's that? Where are you going?" I mean, driving me fuckin' nuts. It especially got bad when my new girlfriend moved in. I wound up letting a couple of friends move in, and one night, a female friend brought these two girls over. Both were seventeen, and I was in my twenties. I have tried dating women my age many times. Obviously, I didn't look my age. I was at a bar with a couple of friends once and checking out a lady around my age. I told the waitress I wanted to buy her whatever she was drinking, and she came over to our table and thanked me for the drink. She couldn't accept it because she had a kid who was my age. Boy, was I offended. I told her, "Lady, I guarantee you don't. I'm actually probably older than you." It seriously pissed me off no matter how hard I tried. The only females interested in me were sixteen to nineteen, and sixteen was definitely too young. These girls were just a few weeks from turning eighteen. Lucky for me the hottest one was the one who liked me. I was sitting on my weight bench with her in front of me. She kept leaning back into me after we had a few drinks. I asked if she wanted to go for a ride. Lynn's mother living next door was always nosing around. As the hot girl and I were walking out to the car, Marie started fighting, asking me, "Who is this girl." I told her none of her business, so of course, she started yelling at the hottie, calling her names, so this girl wanted to know who that was. I just said long story. We just drove around the block, found a dark spot, and parked. Boy, Oh boy! what a night that turned out to be; wow! As a matter of fact, I wound up being with her for over four years.

Jimmy, Marie's boyfriend, was working with me on a house I'd been trying to finish for a while. The problem was it was near the end of winter, and the weather was not cooperating. The roof was really steep, so no walking on that bad baby. I had Jimmy finishing up on the capping, and I had one valley I needed to cut. A valley is where the roof comes together from two different angles, and there was still quite a bit of snow on it. It was supposed to be sunny the following day. I thought if I kicked off as much snow as possible, I might get lucky and have the sun melt the rest as I was kicking the snow. I was getting quite a bit of it, then whoops! I started to lose my grip, and at the place where Jimmy was capping, all he had to do was get up and walk toward me with the air hose connected to the nail gun, and then I could just grab onto the air hose and not fall. I started hollering for him to quickly get up and bring the nail gun toward me. He's panicking, and instead of getting up and walking my way. He unhooked the hose from the gun and threw it. Like I was gonna catch it and what! Follow it to the ground? I don't know what he was thinking, but he threw my chance to avoid falling right down the roof. The next thing I know, his feet are above my head, and he's yelling grab my legs.

I'm like. "Dude, I can't grab your legs; the second I let go, I'm gone." I thought, well, I had no choice but to try. Just like I thought, I went for a ride the second I let go. I felt like I was a bobsled. I shot off the roof like a bullet landing on a pile of bricks. Lying there mustering up the words OOWWW. I could hear Jimmy yelling, "KENNYY!" I thought fuck him; he can think I'm dead. I could hear him climbing down the ladder practically in tears repeating, "oh my god! I fuckin' killed him! Oh my god!" The first thing I said to him was, "Fucker, you threw my lifeline down the roof; why?" I also let him explain to my girlfriend as to why I was fucked up.

CHAPTER 18

Having Marie living next door was a constant battle. She brought Lynn over one day as we were standing talking in the drive. Slamming the baby on the hood of my car like a fucktard telling me it was time to watch my kid. *Did she think the baby was a suitcase to be slamming around?* I wanted to slam her around the same way. Her boyfriend Jimmy I actually liked. He was starting to see how she truly was. A nut case and decided to get out while he had the chance. Around the same time Larry left me, I bumped into an old friend from way back, and he had been doing roofing as well. I thought what a coincidence we joined up and started working together. Putting both our talents together worked out pretty well for both of us. What I didn't know, he knew how to do and vice versa. Plus, I was financially in better shape and good with customer relations. It was a good combo, and we did some amazing jobs. I've had up to three jobs going at the same time. I once had this roof in Fenton, which was an add-on to a log cabin, and I had another in Flint I was doing at the same time. I had to go to Fenton first and get my crew going on the addition. I had to check on the other crew in Flint. After I left for Flint, the painters had brushed varnish on the fascia, which is the spot where your gutter goes, and when I got back, I didn't know about the varnish. One of my rules was never to come up empty-handed, especially if shingles are on the ground.

I walked over and grabbed one, threw it on my shoulder, and started up the ladder. I was right at the top when I started to flip the bundle over, and when I did, the ladder slipped on the varnish and went sideways on me. I did a flip with the bundle on my shoulder and somehow landed right across the windowsill below me on my ribs. Thank God there was no window; I would have been killed. The homeowner and the builder were standing just inside. After sliding off the windowsill, I dropped to the floor and grabbed my stomach. As the builder was asking me, are you okay? I couldn't say anything for a minute. I was still trying to breathe, and my ribs hurt like hell. I almost puked. I wound up cracking two of my ribs, but I did finish working that day. Afterward, I hurt too bad even to drive, so one of my guys drove to the job in Flint and had them call it a day. The next few days were horrible. I hurt so bad I could barely move. I had to just supervise from the ground. The messed-up part is this happened right in front of my girlfriend, who was coming up the ladder behind me.

My new girlfriend was a tough girl even though she didn't look like it. She actually had the guts to go on to a lot of my jobs. One particular job was a huge apartment building. It was so tall I didn't have a ladder tall enough to reach it. We had to climb through the rafters to get onto the roof. That job took a long time to do. I had difficulty finding people willing to get on it; it was the biggest roof I'd ever done. When they brought the materials, the conveyor barely reached the bottom. We all had to catch everything at the bottom. A conveyor truck has rubber paddles that will carry a bundle of shingles from the truck to the roof. Watching these guys who were scared trying to grab these bundles was truly funny and annoying at the same time. I mean, my girlfriend was grabbing bundles and carrying them to the guys, who were too scared to walk close to the bottom. I wonder if they were embarrassed by a chic who was braver than they were. One guy was so scared he scooted around on his ass.

When we would get new guys, we always liked fucking with them. Sending them down for board stretchers or a left-handed hammer. Most of them were gullible enough to go look for one. Stevie, one of my old friends, sent a guy clear across the subdivision for a board stretcher. I heard him giggling and said, "What are you laughing about?" He said, "I sent the new guy for a board stretcher." Sometimes we just didn't have time for that shit. We were trying to finish the job and not send our gopher on a goose chase. I had to holler for him. He couldn't hear me, so I hollered at my partner to call him back. John had no idea where he was going; he yelled, "HEY! WHERE ARE YOU GOING?" He started trying to explain where he was going. John just yelled, "GET BACK HERE!" Stevie laughed the whole time. I had to explain to the new guy he was being fucked with. McCall would mess with people so bad that he was chasing off the help. Twice he made guys so upset they walked off the job. One guy walked nearly ten miles to get back to his car and refused to work with us again.

I had this guy I had done a few roofs for. He showed up at my house one day. He was throwing this idea about partnering up with him and his friend George. George's father had passed and left him the family business, and he just needed someone like me to help him out. I thought it was a great opportunity. He owned a pretty good-sized building with huge contracts with many builders building these huge subdivisions with homes, ranging from two hundred and fifty to six hundred thousand dollars. He even had a conveyor truck to deliver the material on top of the roof, delivering the materials to his building straight from the manufacturer. Needless to say, he had a hell of a thing going. At first, things were going pretty well. Then George just wanted to play with his quads, jet skis, and boats. This was a pretty big business. He was supposed to give me access to the contracts and builders and support my decisions with the roofing and siding crews. They would not consider me their boss. We needed to have meetings and such to run the business. One night I came by the office to fix some lights on our trailer I was hauling, and every light in the building was on, including the offices. Also, the front door was wide open.

I was pissed off, to say the least. I told them to get the fuck out of there. They said George told them they could stay in the loft upstairs. I tried reaching George on the phone with no luck. Then they started telling me about a fight they got into with a guy at the store around the corner. One of them bit the guy's ear off. I'm thinking, *what the fuck? You bring your fuckin asses back here, so the law will look for you here, great!* I went back to the loading dock and told my guy's let's get these lights fixed and get the fuck outta here. I don't want to be here when the cops show up. The next thing I knew, I looked up, and one of those idiots went running like hell through the dock; I thought, too late. The cops were already there. I explained the best I could as to who I was to the company, and I had nothing to do with what those fools had done. Not being able to get a hold of George was not helping. Luckily, I could find his mother's number, which I now wished I would have held onto because I had decided I was done trying to work with George. Had I kept his mom's number, she would have let me take the business over, and it would have never gone out of business.

I had my business for nearly seventeen years. I've got so many stories I could write three books. I've had quite a few guys who have worked for me through the years with some odd names. I've had a Harry Dick, Gay Host, and even a Brent Dick take out the R, and what do you get? There was this guy Ben Dover. I shit you not, that was his name. One of my other rules was: if you're carrying a bundle of shingles and drop them, don't try and catch them; let it go. I can replace shingles; I can't replace you but make sure you holler heads up or something to let the people below you know something is coming. Ole Ben was carrying up some shingles, and of course, he dropped a bundle. The roof we were doing had a huge side with a lot of squares.

Meaning it's big, so as the bundle is sliding down the roof, Ben was on his ass sliding right behind, yelling," OH WATCH OUT! OH WATCH OUT," over and over. As they were sliding, I saw the bundle go bye, and here comes Ben. I reached out and grabbed him by his shirt. You should have seen his eyes. I thought he was gonna shit his pants. My first couple of years of roofing beat me up a bit. I remember waking up the following morning, barely able to open my hands. It seemed as if every job

I was getting was a nasty-ass cedar shake tear-off with like four fucking layers of shingles. For those who don't know what cedar shakes are, they're wooden shingles used during the depression. Saving money on wood and then just kept laying shingles over the top. Before my split with Larry, we had done a job for this contractor, and we told him it was a cedar shake roof and the law required him to lay plywood over the planks. Mr. Tightwad didn't want to spend the extra money.

After Larry and I were no longer working together, Mr. Tightwad called me saying, "Uh, remember the certain roof you told me we had to sheet? Well, the building inspector says we have to redo it." Laughing, I asked him, "isn't that what we told you?" Not that he wanted to hear me say that, but he couldn't get anyone else to do it. He had to pay me to tear off the brand-new shingles, lay the plywood, and re-shingle. It was one expensive lesson to learn. He should have done it right the first time, which is a great rule. The worst part was we had to do it in the winter. After getting it halfway done, the temperature took a deep dive. It was so cold you could barely walk a block without freezing. I needed to get this job done. We went out with about four layers of clothes on. We had just finished sheeting one side, and I started laying down ice and water shield at the bottom of the roof. I had to do it by standing on the ladder of a two-story building as I started to lay out the ice and water. I had a guy on the roof helping me because of the wind. Without warning, the ladder slipped out from under me.

As I'm riding the ladder down. My first thought was *oh shit, I'm fucked not getting this job done today.* I bounced off the ladder, then once more off the ground. I immediately stood up like a badass. ROAR! Which didn't work out very well because I immediately fell down again. My legs hurt like hell, and my guy is still on the roof. He was looking down and yelling, "HEY! How am I getting down?" No way could I put the ladder back up. Luckily, I had a few youngsters cleaning up the ground. I had to coach them on how to get the ladder back up for Rick. I nearly broke my legs. They hurt so bad I got home and got undressed. The front of my legs was skinned nearly to the bone. Of course, I had to take some time off for that one. I was a bit picky from that point on. I would have someone standing at the bottom of the ladder, making sure it stayed put. I wasn't taking any chances! It didn't stop me; I had to fall off a few more roofs. The luck I had in my life called for a few more. What I thought was weird was I was hurt worse by the shortfalls. Like I fell off a porch once and received more injuries than I did from falling two stories.

You would think that I would just quit as often as I've fallen off roofs, stapling my knee crack, ribs, cutting my fingers and hands—the job where ole Ben Dover nearly slid off with a bundle of shingles. I was about to nail a two-by-four down to the roof. Hammering a sixteen-penny spike into the roof, and as I'm hammering, I wound up hitting the wrong nail—God damn fingernail. I didn't even feel it. It was like hitting a grape; blood squirted all over my glasses. My first thought was, *what the hell was that?* Until I looked down and saw what was left of my finger. My next thought was, *holy shit, I just squashed my fucking finger.* I jumped up and yelled, "McCall! Look at what the fuck I just did! Talk about pain. I just smashed my index finger on my left hand, my nail-holding finger. I hurried up and went to the ground, looking for running water. I ran my finger under the water for about an hour, took some Tylenol, and taped it up with black tape. Then I went back to work using my middle finger to hold my nails. Believe it or not, I didn't even lose my fingernail; it hurt for a long ass time. I got so used to using my middle finger to hold my nails. It was almost hard to go back to using the index.

CHAPTER 19

As we all know, Ric he's a little guy. We had this job and had just finished tearing it off and ready for shingling when a storm started to blow out of nowhere. We were hurrying to get it covered with a tarp, and the section we covered was pretty big. Suddenly, the wind picked up, and I mean literally picked Ric up. He was at the bottom corner, and the tarp started to take Ric for a ride. Ric would have flown away if we hadn't had a good hold. His feet were nearly six feet from the roof.

Doing another Flint job, the jobs were always fucked up in Flint. We could see the storm coming, so we got the top covered, but right under the dormer was a section that had come loose. A dormer is a little hard to explain, but it's a small roof that is on the main roof. It was freaking pouring rain capable of washing your car away. We got up there to fix the one section but couldn't get it to stay. I had to stand there holding the tarp in place through the whole fuckin' storm. I was completely soaked. I was so wet the water squished from my shoes when I walked. We had a lot of them staying on the roof during a storm. I was already home once, and we were watching the weather channel, and they were talking about a bad storm heading towards my job. It was just Jay and me when we showed up. It was a light rain, so we stapled down two tarps. After getting down, the damn wind blew up two areas of the tarp. We quickly got back up; no matter what we did, we could not get the areas to stay down. The wind and rain were so hard, that Jay and I had to scream to hear each other.

I sat on the one spot, he sat on the other, and we just rode the storm out. We were just screaming, "This ain't no fucking storm!" Yes, it most definitely was, but it was our way of toughing it out. The 1990s was one strange decade not just because of the war; there were blowjobs, and Mickey mouse club kids were becoming big stars. 1997 was a good year for business. My life was going pretty well. I had a beautiful girlfriend. Good kid. I loved the home we had. We bought a house on the east side from my sister and Bud, my brother-in-law. Bud and I had even done some work together. My sister and I had a good relationship as well. I made a mistake by putting my business on the yellow pages. My phone was ringing off the hook. I should have hired more crews and possibly a secretary, but unfortunately, I wasn't that smart. I had so much work I was moving my ladder from one house to another without having to put it on the van. One August evening, I got a call from my grandpa's oldest son's wife. Telling me, he had been missing since the night before; my first thought was maybe he found a piece on the side. It was something out of the ordinary for him. I asked, "Did you guys have an argument or something?"

She said They weren't having any problems; everything was great. His son was about to start kindergarten and was excited about taking his boy for his first day of school." I knew he wouldn't miss that. I said, "Just tell him to call me when he does get home or if in a couple of days you still haven't heard from him, call me back."

Sure enough, they called me back a few days later with still no word. I started to get worried. It was not like him just to disappear. I drove to Owosso and talked with everyone there who said he had gone to the bar with the guy upstairs. He never came home, and the guy upstairs was telling conflicting stories. I went upstairs to talk to this guy. I was told his name was Bob. When I knocked on the door, the guy inside yelled, "Yeah." I asked, "Are you, Bob?" The strange response was, "I used to be."

Okay, what a weird thing to say, I was thinking. I walked in, introduced myself, and said, "I want to hear your side of what happened." I wasn't going just to assume everyone was telling the truth until I got his side. Immediately he came across with a serious attitude and told me he was tired of explaining and that he didn't have to explain himself to anyone. "I don't give a shit what you're tired of; you're going to tell me something whether you like it or not!" I told him. He suddenly reached out, poked me in the chest, and started yelling, Well, that didn't go over too well for him. I grabbed him by his throat and slammed him onto his couch. He jumped up to try and fight back. By this time, I had snapped. This time I just started wailing on him, grabbing his throat again. I had him pinned on the couch and kept wailing on him. He started yelling for my friend, Roberto, to help him. He was asking the wrong guy. Roberto was my friend, and on my side, so he told ole Bob, "You had better tell him something. I know Kenny, and when he's pissed, he's not gonna stop."

Bob started talking, telling me about when they were at the bar. My cousin was on the phone arguing with someone, and when he hung up, he went straight outside. The two of them had ridden bikes to the bar, and when he started to follow my cousin, he was already down the road heading toward home. I told him, "I will believe your story for now, but if I find out you are lying, I'm coming back, and I won't be as nice."

As I started walking down the stairs, he ran out and started yelling names at me. I turned to go back upstairs, and he ran inside and slammed the door. What I thought, a pussy. As I approached the bottom, another guy just pulled in with a truck. Bob came running back out, yelling for his friend to kick my ass. I looked at the friend and asked, "You want any?" The guy just put his hands up and said, "I don't have a problem."

Some old lady living in the building next door lived on the same floor as Bob and could see me whipping his ass called the cops and said I had a knife, so my friend and I were walking to go to the bar where they had gone to get some information. The next thing I knew, I was being surrounded by cop cars like they were SWAT scared the shit out of me. Pulling guns and slammed me into the car. Confused as to what in the hell was going on. I started asking, "What is this for?" After explaining what the old lady had said. I told them, "I never pulled a knife. It was a straight-up fight."

Believe it or not, they waited to find out if he was going to press charges. It turned out he was a bigger man than I thought. No charges. But some fag in Flint wanted to press charges for an ass whipping he received a few years back. Them fuckers arrested me for that. Luckily, I had my girl with me, and she bailed me out. The guy who did press charges; what a pussy; the little thief stole two of my nail guns off my kitchen table as he left my house. The dumb cock sucker was stupid enough to try and sell them to my friend. What a dumb ass he knew this guy, and I had a past. We had been friends for a long time. Like he wasn't going to come to me and tell me who stole them. Of course, he did, and when I saw the little thief a few months later, I kicked the shit out of him with my bro, Ric. One of the nail guns belonged to him. It was the way things were done when I was younger; you fuck up, you get fucked up, and you don't cry to the cops like a bitch. After getting bailed out, I searched with family and friends for my cousin. I even called some television stations to get his story on T.V.

I put his picture out with the fliers I had made up, giving a description of him and the bike he was on. The police aren't helping for shit either. I was fighting with the detectives. Trying to get them to do their fuckin job, useless bastards. The funny thing is those bastards found his bike two weeks after he was reported missing and did not inform us, which would have been helpful. When they found his body nearly eight months later, it wasn't but two hundred yards away from where they found his bike, and they didn't think to search the area. Or tell us so we could? They also found his glasses a mile away. The funny thing was ole Bob told me he was headed toward home the last he saw him. His body was found nearly three miles in the opposite direction, and he was found by an employee of the Owosso Country Club because his body was on the country club's property. On the golf course of all places. When I went there to talk with the employees, they informed me the club was open until November that year because we had such a warm Autumn.

Since he had been missing since August, there was no way he lay there dead from August to November without someone smelling a dead body. The police also said he fell down a sixty-foot embankment and was close to the water. There was no such embankment, nor was he near any water. He was lying at the bottom of a small hill nearly three hundred yards from any water. Losing my cousin in such a way broke my heart. He had been in my life as far back as I can remember. He wasn't just my cousin to me; he was my little brother. There was nothing I could do to bring him justice. I had a business and two children of my own to think about. I didn't have the time or the money to spare to get the justice he deserved. His wife had already moved on before knowing whether he was dead or not. The day we arranged for his funeral, she was dancing to the music in her car. My Aunt Berta had already spent all the money my grandfather left her when he passed on his eighty-fourth birthday; what *a strange day to die the same day he was born.* So no one had any money to put toward a decent burial except for his mother-in-law and me. I wasn't about to let my little brother be buried in a cardboard box, so I paid out what I had to. I couldn't get justice, but I made sure he was laid to rest properly. The worst thing was I lost my grandfather not two years before. *Strangely they both died in the same month, just two years apart.*

I've already mentioned a few of my many jobs. I could tell story after story about my business. I even went incorporated once, even though it didn't work out as planned. I gave it one hell of a shot. Instead of spending my money correctly, I blew it like a dumb ass. I wish I had someone to guide me a little. My father was no help for sure, and my grandpa was too busy with his tards.

It was about to turn the year 2000, and the world was flipping out. Everyone was thinking, OH NO! What are we going to do? The computers are going to shut everything down. They didn't think the world's computers would recognize the new year. Everyone bought up everything in the stores from food, too, you name it. *I personally believe it was a way to make people ridiculously spend their money.* They did. Prince even wrote a song about it, referring to the thought that the world's nuclear bombs would automatically lift off, and 1999 was the last year to dance and party. At eleven fifty-nine on New Year's Eve 1999, we all just prayed the lights would stay on, and there was no end to the world. *I thought it was silly for people to worry about such a thing. People are so gullible they believe the craziest things.* All the government has to do is say it, and the people go OOOHHHH!!

CHAPTER 20

A few years after burying my cousin, my girlfriend and I broke up. I was trying to win her back, but whenever I thought we were getting somewhere, she would pull back. My birthday came around, and I was hoping to spend it with her. We went to my mom's and stepdad's house. I believe I drank a bit too much. We went back to the house where I was hoping to get lucky, and she wasn't being very cooperative. Standing by the back door, I was lightly punching a shatter less window, so much for being shatterproof. This fucking thing shattered and somehow slit my left wrist; blood squirted everywhere. I was completely panicked. Luckily, she did not. She quickly grabbed a towel and applied pressure, hoping to stop or even slow it down. No such luck; I thought *for sure this was it. I was going to bleed to death.* She rushed me into the car and called my sister by the time we reached the hospital. Bud was at the car door, grabbing me and running inside with a trail of blood. The nurses thought I had tried to commit suicide, so they were not being very nice to me. I kept telling them it was an accident. I don't think they believed me because I nearly cut my artery in half. They stitched me up and let me go.

I was in the middle of a roofing job too. Luckily, I was good friends with the homeowner, and he cut me some slack.

In the year 2000, we had a cluster-fuck of an election for our president George W fuckin' Bush. Florida had a real problem with their state's election count, and it was to the point that whoever won that state would be the next president. Of course, the governor of Florida just happened to be related to ole George. The economy had gotten so bad that people were committing suicide because they couldn't afford to keep their homes. He was the worst president I can ever remember, *besides the idiot, we have now*. George W Bush walked into the White House to literally fuck this country. This guy should have never had the opportunity to be the president. He escaped a dishonorable discharge because of who his daddy was. When you have orders you're supposed to follow twice, he fell short of meeting his military requirements, once in May of 1968 and again in mid-1973. He didn't meet his commitments or face any punishment.

I know he tried more than once to allow Mexican drivers from Mexico to drive into our country, basically to take American jobs. I almost believed he was anti-American. He drove us into a recession. September 11, 2001, at approximately eight forty-six in the morning. A Boeing 767 loaded with twenty thousand gallons of jet fuel flew into one of the twin towers in New York City. Then seventeen minutes later, another plane hit the other tower. It was considered the worst terrorist attack in U.S. history. The impact left a burning hole near the eightieth floor, killing hundreds of people and leaving everyone above trapped where people were actually jumping to their deaths. These animals were not done there; around nine thirty-seven am, a third plane crashed into the west side of the Pentagon in Virginia. A fourth plane crashed in Pennsylvania because the brave men and women on that plane took action. They stopped these sick people and caused the plane to crash, killing everyone on board. *I personally consider those folks heroes.* There were hundreds of heroes that day who did their best to save as many lives as possible. I was doing a roof on a church when it happened. My father called me to tell me about the first plane. Of course, I wasn't sure whether to believe him or not since he was Father Goose, so I turned on the radio, and sure enough. We covered the roof and took the rest of the day off. As I walked into my house, I could see people jumping one after another on the television. All I could do was watch in horror. I could not help myself but shed tears for these poor innocent people. The whole country just fell to its knees and wept. It was the first time this country came together as one. People came from miles away to offer their help in any way they could. No matter their race, they opened their arms to everyone who needed it. My wish for my country is *to open their hearts and arms to the people as they did that day.* It proves everyone can forget their petty differences and remember what we all mean to each other. We lost nearly three thousand people in the attack and hundreds more as time passed from broken hearts and suicide or just lost the battle. We lost fathers, mothers, sons, and daughters because of a group of people who hate our country, and yet we allow these people to remain. We have even removed words like Merry Christmas and our pledge of allegiance in our schools because these people who hate us are offended. I personally feel they should just leave. The piece of shit who funded the whole thing, Osama Bin Laden, wasn't killed for nearly ten years. A guy who needed a kidney dialysis machine avoided our great president George W Bush who couldn't find his ass if his life depended on it. Every time he got close, he would just broadcast it on CNN. Someone would just call him and tell him what was going on. He could just ask, "How do you know?" Their reply would be, "I GOT CABLE!"

It seemed people were so much nicer to one another for a few years, but it didn't last long. Soon everyone just went back to their old hateful selves. Sadly, it takes a tragedy like that to make people open their eyes. As our country started falling into recession, gas prices went sky high (Nowhere near what they are now), but people lost their jobs, and their money got tight. As things got tighter, the harder it was to find work. You can say what you want to about ole Bill Clinton when he was president. I never went without work, and I didn't give a shit where he put his dick. As long as the country was thriving, that should have been what mattered. I went from having two to three jobs a week to maybe two to three jobs a month. It was time to start thinking about another way to pay the bills. I wasn't sure what I should do.

I've done construction for so long; what else was there? I'm no genius, and my money is tight. What else am I good at? I've heard truck drivers make good money, and I can pretty much drive anything, so I checked it out. I've grown accustomed to the kind of money I made. I've never had to worry about work.

I've also gone a long time without a license, driving suspended during my dumb days. I got pulled over once on the freeway in 1996, and when I went to court, the judge said, "How come you don't have a license? You only have these two tickets on your record. I thought, HUH?? I wasn't sure what to say. I thought I had a bunch. He told me to pay for those two tickets, get my license back, and he would drop the ticket I was seeing him for. I did that lickety-split. I was never so happy I was actually driving legally. Funny how little things mean so much. I had always known how to drive a stick shift. So I didn't figure having too much trouble learning how to drive a big truck. I started looking into what the requirements were by the state. It turned out I met all of them. I had never had a D.U.I., never had an accident-causing death, and had held the license long enough. Next, I had to find a school, and luckily I found one that gets you hired before you even go to school as long as you're able to pass. Passing the course wasn't hard, but the next two years were a bitch. My backing up was what I was having the most trouble doing. I had this one delivery in Auburn Hills, Mich. It took me almost an hour before giving up as I was trying to come up with an idea of what to do. I watched this guy pull in, whip up, and back right in. I thought, holy shit, he just backed in like it was no problem. I asked him if he would be willing to back my truck into the dock. He said yes, so I paid attention to how he did it because there was no one to help the second time.

CHAPTER 21

I met a lady in late 2001 and wish now I had not. I have always had the worst luck when it came to women. It seems I always wind up in a bad situation. The only child I should have had was Koler. I'm not saying I don't love all my children; I just wish they would have been mothered by someone else. Lynn's mother thought of getting pregnant that maybe I would marry her. No way Jose. The next one was the same way. This was my third child, who turned out to be a boy. I was happy at the thought of having a son. Whose mother once he was born completely changed. She went from being a good homemaker keeping my home clean to making sure there was dinner when I came home. To being filthy, no dinner. I had to start making my own and she also thought she was Leon Spinks, who is a boxer by the way. We had gotten into a few spats before, but this time she was all out for the championship. That was where I drew the line. I refused to be in a violent relationship. I had two daughters who did not deserve to see violence in their homes. I saw it and lived it as a kid. I would never let my kids see or live it. It was over and before my son was born she told me the only way she would give my son my last name is if I married her. I played along for a bit until after he was born. Once the violence started, I refused to even be in any sort of relationship. Again I was not the type to throw my son into the streets. I told her to get a place to go and

I would help of course financially. She would go here and there but would always have to come back. Once I started driving over the road. I was never home anyway so I just let them stay and would only have to put up with her for a couple of days when I would come home.

Again the house was always filthy. I cannot stand filth. Plus her brother had been sitting on the edge of my bed and ruined my brand-new mattress. Not to mention that's where she slept. When I would come home, I still wound up sleeping in my truck. I wound up making her leave because I couldn't take coming home to such a dirty place. Even that turned out to be a mistake because after getting my house nice and cleaned up. While I was out on the road a family just helped themselves to move into my house. They are called squatters and there was nothing I could do but to go to court and evict them. By the time I got them out, my house was destroyed. It seemed I wasn't able to make any good decisions lately! I gave up the whole idea of keeping a house. I just figured she needed to do something on her own. I would just rent a hotel and a car during my home time.

About five months into driving for the first company I received a call from my mom telling me I need to call my dad if I ever wanted to talk to him again. He didn't have long to live; my first thought was sure. If I had a dollar for every time, I've heard that I'd be rich. She said, "No, seriously. I talked with him. Trust me It's for real." I called, and when he got on the phone, I could tell right away she was right. The way he talked I knew I had better get home or he would be dead before I had a chance to say what I'd waited to say for a long time. I needed him to know what he had done to my life. By the time I got to my mom's, I was exhausted. I called him to say I would be there the following morning because I was tired from driving. The following morning I woke up to my mom telling me it was too late. He had died in the night. I felt so cheated. I had things I wanted to say. I said, "Let's go there anyway."

He had died at home so when I got there, I sat with him in the room where he died. I was so angry. I stood up and punched him, in tears asking him why he couldn't have waited one more day. I finally broke down and cried, after everything he had done to me. I'm crying because even though he had hurt me badly. He was still my father and all the shit I had lived through made me who I am. I have made my mistakes but I felt I was a good father and a good man I have always financially supported my family. He and I had a conversation once he apologized for being such a shitty father. He asked me not to let anyone cremate him. The whole thought of being burned terrified him and I totally forgot that conversation. That is exactly what my stepmom did. She had him cremated and it kills my heart to know I didn't stop it.

As I went back to work it was all I could think about. One time I had Lynn with me and we were in Chicago at the Betty Crocker plant. It was so fuckin hot outside I could barely breathe. They wanted me to back in a garage-type dock I couldn't see shit it was like backing into a black hole. I had one truck on my left side and then a huge support beam on the passenger side. As I was backing in, I wasn't able to see I was backing at an angle. I was almost in and wham I wasn't sure what I had hit. I was hoping it was the dock I hit the trailer next to me and broke his trailer door off on the passenger side. After the driver finished yelling at me, I quickly pulled out, a bit pissed off. The next thing I knew wham, I hit the support beam on my passenger door and broke the same fuckin door off. I was not having a good day here. I broke off the same trailer door on two different trailers. I was seriously thinking of quitting for the day. Possibly for good like I said the first couple of years sucked. It was also cool as hell. I got to see nearly the entire country except, of course, Alaska or Hawaii. I will tell you no one needs to leave this country to see the beauty. I have seen some of the most beautiful places at just the right time. Then most people will ever see. Driving through northern Washington east at sunrise will make you want to pull over and just look at the sun rising behind the mountains. It's one of the most beautiful sights I have ever seen coming through certain areas of Utah the Mountains of rock are so huge you can look ahead and see the traffic. They look like moving toys there is a scene in the movie Forrest Gump where he's telling Jenny about his travels and he talks about the beauty of looking at the sky, not being able to tell where heaven ends and the earth begins. It is a scene I can relate to because I've seen that very same sight.

In my first year, I was driving through Montana and I could see a large blue lake down the road. Every time I would get to where the lake was supposed to be. No lake. I couldn't figure out if I was hallucinating. As a matter of fact, I was, I could see so far ahead it looked as if the sky was lying on the ground. I was amazed at how blue the sky really was. I even took Koler and Lynn with me one at a time, of course, I'm not crazy about having two girls in the truck for nearly a month. Koler always wanted to go to California and just as I would drop her back at home. I would get a load to California. Boy, did that tick her off one time my truck broke down in western Tennessee so the company put us up in a motel with a pool for nearly a week. Koler would not get out of the pool. I thought she was going to turn into a fish she did avoid that part but wound up with a horrible ear infection instead. I felt so bad for her while she cried I tried buying everything I could think of to help her. Until someone told me about a home remedy which I thought was pretty gross. My mom tells me to let her pee in a cup and pour it in her ear. Neither one of us was keen on that idea but we had tried everything else. So we gave the ridiculous a try, believe it or not, it worked. I couldn't believe it I was completely shocked, I would have had to take her to a doctor if she didn't get better. Koler kept falling asleep sitting in the passenger seat and I needed her awake to help me stay awake. What a jerk I was I looked over and she was totally out so I hit the brakes and started screaming. I thought I was going to have to pry her fingernails out of the ceiling. I laughed so hard I could hardly breathe; she wasn't amused I have no idea why lol. If looks could kill, it would have been my last day.

CHAPTER 22

Lynn had a hard time waking up in the morning to climb to the bottom bed. After I woke up, I would say, "Hey, Lynn wake up and get on the bottom bunk." "Okay," is what she'd say, but never got up. I would normally drive through the cities in the morning getting ready to either pick up or deliver. People forget how to drive sometimes and I would have to hit the brakes. Next thing I know, here comes Lynn flying off the bed, WHAM! On the floor she slams, then she's mad at me I told you to get up, not my fault you didn't get up. I've told her many times being on the top bunk is not a good idea when the truck is moving. Especially when there's a step down to enter the sleeper area. Sure enough, she hit that damn step. OW! I know it had to hurt; She hurt her back falling so luckily I had some Tylenol. One bad thing about driving a big truck is when you have to use the John, you can't just pull into a gas station or Burger King. You need serious room and I was on the freeway in PA once I had to go number two so bad I was squirming in the driver's seat hoping to see a truck stop. Finally, I saw one just a few miles away by this time, I was praying to the poo-poo god to please let me make it. Just as I pulled in, I pulled the air brakes and as the brakes released the air, the poo poo god thought it would be funny to release something of its own. I however did not find it very funny, I immediately jumped out yelling for Koler to please bring me some underpants. As I flew into the restroom thanking god there was a stall available. I have no idea what I would have done had there been no stall I think I would have killed someone. As I'm cleaning myself up bitching out the poo-poo god severely I hear Koler open the door and yell, "Here Dad, your underwear!" . I shrank so small I could literally walk under the stall without even bending over. I hollered out, "SHHH! QUIET! I'll be right there."

I waited for everyone to leave the bathroom before coming out to this day we still laugh about it. I was forced to give up my construction company and start driving a semi in 2004. Later this same year my brother-in-law, Bud had a car accident injuring his back in several places. Pinching a nerve in his leg took him from being able to do full-time work to never working again. Causing them to go into financial trouble but were able to get their lawyer to work it out, but not before losing their home they were forced to move up north into a cabin.

It was hard being by myself all the time. I was lonely. I had never been good with having no one to talk to. I found myself just striking up a conversation with anyone willing to talk. I loved traveling and my job. I just didn't want to do it by myself. Somehow, I met another problem. *Now you want to talk about the worst women, this bitch took the cake.* She was good for a while because she went with me on the road. At least I wasn't alone, but then she was getting tired of the road and started doing dumb shit during our home time. Until one time we had come home for Christmas I always came home to spend it with my kids, and it was time to go back to work. I had a load already in my trailer I was supposed to deliver a few days later. She asked if she could go say goodbye to her mom and grab a few things from the store before leaving the following morning. Of course, I had no problem with it I liked her mom and she didn't live far. I gave her money and my keys. The bitch never came back. I was so fucking pissed. I didn't know what to do. Not only did she have my vehicle but my wallet and the keys to my semi. I wasn't able to go anywhere and had to call my job to get someone else to grab my trailer to make the delivery. I even called the cops, there was nothing they could do since I let her take it. I found her two days later at her mom's. She did have my wallet with no money, of course, but no van. She told me where the van was and what apartment the guy was in who had the keys. She owed him money he said no money, no keys. I had to have my neighbor take me to get my wallet from her and find out where my van was. As we were backing out of the drive, she said to me, "What no hug?" I thought *are you fucking crazy? Hug? Bitch you're lucky I don't bust your fucking teeth out.* My van happened to be at an apartment complex that was one hundred percent black. I pounded on the guy's door yelling I wanted the keys to my van. No one answered the door. I went outside screaming like a madman, "Nigger, you better bring my keys out or I will fucking kick your door in." Remember this is the way I was taught, the biker way I never took shit from anyone. I didn't care what color they were or how big they were. I have never been scared of anyone and never will be. I was screaming nigger over and over I literally was so mad I lost my mind. A bunch of people was looking out the window even approaching me, I seriously didn't give a fuck. I even attacked a few guys which made my neighbor leave me. I have no idea what I was thinking he said, "I thought you were going to be killed." Finally, the guy who had my keys stuck his head out of his window and told me to go fuck myself I wasn't getting shit. That bitch owes me money and until I get it you ain't getting no keys. I told him, "Nigger, I'm going to tell you one more time. I don't owe you shit and if you don't give me my keys. I'm going to jump up there grab you by your nigger throat and pull you out of that window. I promise I will kill you." He didn't, believe me, he started to say, "I would love to see you try." Before he could finish his sentence, I ran over, jumped up, grabbed his air conditioner to pull myself up further, and DID!! grab him by the throat. No sooner than I grabbed him someone threw my keys into my chest. I let him go, yelled some more, and left telling him how lucky he was. I seriously would have killed him. I had completely snapped the thing is I'm not prejudiced against color. I was just so mad I wanted to hurt someone and didn't care who. I have snapped like this before and it scares me when I do because I know I'm capable of killing someone when it happens. I once did that to a woman who came to my house and pulled a knife on my wife. I came out of the house and grabbed her by the throat and nearly drowned her in my basement which was full of water at the time. I had what they called a Michigan basement and for some reason, it kept filling up with water. I was screaming the whole time about bringing a knife. I didn't mind them fighting. It just needed to be without a weapon. After pulling her out of the water and still having her by the throat. She grabbed both hands full of my hair which didn't phase me at all, slamming her down on the ground. I let go of her throat and put my fingers around her face squeezing. Finally, Ric grabbed me. Thank God he did. As soon as I had calmed down, I started to cry I couldn't believe I had snapped I seriously could have killed her I felt horrible. This was a woman. *Was I more like my father than I thought?* The thought of me snapping at a woman like that. I would never forgive myself. I swore I would never let that happen again and to this day I never have. I once even snapped like that on my dad which I should have done long ago but he collapsed on the floor because he stopped breathing. I was holding him in a full nelson, this is where you're standing behind someone with your arms underneath theirs and having locked your fingers behind the neck. After he collapsed on the floor, I immediately went to his aid feeling like crap for hurting him, even though he had done it to me, but then again I'm not him.

CHAPTER 23

I met another lousy choice online this time, everyone was using computers and laptops. I didn't know much about them but figured I should try and keep up. I believe somehow, I was able to magnetically attract the worst women. Thank God she wasn't able to have any more kids. At first, I thought she was a real catch. I should have done a catch and release. She had this guy friend from down the road who turned out to be her boyfriend. They decided to play some games online, bringing me into the picture. *What the real endgame was I have no clue.* He wound up losing out completely because she chose me over him. I didn't find all this out until we were near the end. Believe me when I say if a woman says she has a guy friend. Unless he's gay he's not a friend. I guarantee you, there fuckin.'

I thought maybe I could get a local job to get to know this lady better and see my kids more often. My son's mother had gotten married and had a daughter, but I guess her new husband had gotten himself into some trouble and went to prison. She moved to Saginaw bouncing from place to place. The next thing I heard she was staying at a shelter. There was no way I was going to let my son live that way. I took custody of my son, which wasn't much of a problem because, she was homeless. Koler was staying with my mom going to school because of the driving job I couldn't have her with me all the time.

Lynn was living with her mom. I didn't have custody of her. I didn't like having Koler living with my mom. Not that I didn't trust my mom but she was living up north which made it difficult for me to see her. I wasn't ready to just move my kids and myself into this lady's place.

I did however have to bring my son there no judge was going to give me custody of my son driving over the road. Once he started school, they were having trouble with his behavior he was even hitting the other kids and even bit his teacher. I had no idea how to handle the situation Koler or Lynn had never behaved this way. I did what I always have done I lit his little ass on fire hoping he would change his behavior nope didn't work. I even had to quit working to go to his school to babysit him I was completely beside myself this was not a long-term solution. I could not be going to school with him every day. I was already dealing with my new girl and her bratty-ass kids. Not to mention I've been getting calls from guys telling me she's been cheating. I was getting stressed out and my blood pressure was out of control. I developed a cough I could not get rid of. Between her brats and her ex, and the phone calls. I couldn't take it anymore. I wound up moving to my mom's and went back to driving. By this time I was convinced I did not want another woman in my life. I had already screwed up enough. I decided to just date here and there when I was able. After moving to my mom's, Koler had taken over caring for my son and he was doing so much better at school. I had come to the conclusion he had ADHD. Later finding out he was even autistic which explained his behavior somewhat. I felt he should be able to have more control of himself

In 2011, I was working for a company that wanted me to start training drivers. I took the class and passed with flying colors and they gave me a brand-new truck. My first student was an older lady who smoked cigarettes, which I didn't mind but this woman smoked like a house on fire. While she was supposed to be sleeping, she was spending time on the phone. She was just days away from graduating and me getting this bitch out of my truck. We were coming from Arizona making a partial delivery in Dallas and final delivery in Houston with another load to pick up in Houston, taking us to Chattanooga, TN to test her out and get rid of her finally and I couldn't wait. We fueled up just inside Texas and then it was her turn to start driving. She got her logs caught up and started driving. I went in the back to sleep. I was sound asleep; she had only been driving for four hours. The next thing I know I felt a huge pain and loud crashing noises. Shit flying around. I even got hit with my television. This bitch fell asleep at the wheel and ran into a bridge. Paramedics took me to the hospital. *Can you believe I was the only one who got hurt?* They let me go without giving me anything for pain, my neck hurt so bad I couldn't move. We wound up flying to Nashville, TN. By the time we got there, I was in so much pain, I was crying. This was on a Sunday. I bought some Advil which I was eating like candy. Monday morning I went to the main terminal and got set up with a job. While you are on workman's comp, they give you a job to do at the main terminal. They gave me a check so I could get some clothes and a few items because everything I owned was in the truck. Tuesday morning I could not get up. I could barely move without tears. Another driver came into my room and helped me up. He told me I didn't look good at all and called the ambulance. After getting to the hospital, I found out my neck was broken. Broke a piece of bone right off the seventh vertebrae. After getting back from the hospital, I found out that the bitch who nearly killed me, told the lady at the motel she hoped I die; *What the fuck!* She nearly kills me and I'm the bad guy? Turned out she told everyone I forced her to drive even after telling me she was, too tired to drive. I mean seriously bitch? She never said a damn thing about being tired. Like I would want her to drive tired! I would rather be late with delivery than take a chance on this bitch driving tired. After hearing she said she hoped I would die the company gave her a one-way ticket, see ya!

Nearly four and a half months I spent on workman's comp. Working in the log and safety department. Flying me home once a month for home time. Of course, during one of my home times, Koler informs me she's pregnant by the idiot she had been seeing since she was fifteen. I was thrilled, I'm being sarcastic, of course, this guy was the last guy I would want to father my grandchildren. He had as much chance at actually doing something with his life as I do waking up a millionaire. I was not happy, to say the least, but I would love my grandbaby either way.

While waiting for my grandson I was still on the road and the day she had him was such a lucky day for me. I was coming home just in time for them to call and say she was at the hospital. I was so worried I was going to be too far away to make it for the delivery but I was able to drop my trailer and bobtail to the hospital where I got to hold my little girl's hand as she gave birth to my first grandson.

I was so excited I ran out to the lobby to tell everyone the baby was here and ok. I started to run back and Jean yelled out, "Hey, what about our baby?" I thought," OH yeah she's doing great." The nurse thought it was strange for my daughter to want me in the room instead of her mom. Jean told her she was closer to her dad. My grandson was born twelve days after my birthday and afterward, I was so tired from driving and the baby taking so long to come I spent a little time with Koler and the baby but was ready to crash. I went out to the truck and was sawing logs in no time. Bringing the little man home was a happy day. It made me think about the day we brought Koler home. We had been staying with my mom and Glenn during the pregnancy because our house was in no condition to be bringing our baby into. My dad had lived there just before we got married and had left some creepy crawlers behind. We had tried everything to get rid of those little bastards but it seemed they were refusing to move so I had to evict them. I gutted the house and bought a big supply of bug killer ripped out all the cabinets in the kitchen. I sprayed the killer every day for months while repairing everything. I even took the wood from the cabinets and built a baby closet. Just in time, I was so proud of the work I did. I knew my grandma was smiling from the heavens.

We weren't back in the house but maybe a month before baby time. My old friend from the hospital was visiting at the time and as I was running down the road to get my father-in-law to take us to the hospital, he was singing, baby time driving Jean crazy. She told me when I got back don't ever leave her alone with him again. I think it was the labor pains talking., lol.

CHAPTER 24

I met my second wife approximately six months after becoming a grandfather on New Year's Eve in 2012. We brought in the new year together and have been together ever since. It's been over ten years since we met. We have been through a lot together with different disagreements and making up. But she's always had my back; we were married on August 17 and had our reception. Without even changing clothes, we took off to the Woodward Cruise. You wouldn't believe how many people asked did you just get married? *Like, duh, we just hang out in a wedding dress and tuxedo for fun.* Then the next day we went to a Kid Rock concert.

We had gone early and parked. We were the only ones there for nearly an hour and had a few drinks in the parking lot. We had a blast that night and the following morning. We were on the road again. She spent nearly ten months on the road with me; she had never been able to travel like this before, even though she lived in California and New York. She always went by plane, so to be able to travel in such a way was great. We did have some problems with sleeping because the bed wasn't big enough for both of us. We slept opposite with our feet in each other's faces. Thank God neither one of us had stinky feet. One morning I woke up and had this terrible urge to let out a fart. I tried jumping over her as I slept against the back wall. I was trying to avoid farting in her face. As

I jumped, it blew like a bomb. My first thought was, holy shit, I'm sorry. Instead of jumping up and yelling, she lay calmly and said, "YUMMY!" I thought, oh my God, seriously! Later as we were driving down the road, I had to ask, "What in the hell was that YUMMY! Shit about this morning?" It turned out she didn't even remember saying it. We laughed for days about it, and still, sometimes we think back and laugh. We had a lot of times where we would just laugh so hard our stomachs hurt.

One time we were parked, and I was sitting on the bed eating. When the truck next to us was pulling out, for some reason, I thought our truck was rolling backward. I jumped up like a madman jumping in the driver's seat, slamming on the brakes. I nearly broke my fucking knee on the steering wheel jumping in the seat.

We once picked up a load in El Paso, Texas, and were on our way to Dallas. An ice storm was so bad that the freeway had nearly six inches of ice. Trucks were sliding everywhere. It took three days to do a ten-hour trip. Truck stops were running out of fuel, and the restaurants were running out of food. It was horrible. Luckily, we had enough food and water to get us through, and I was smart enough to fill up with fuel at our last stop. They had drivers fist fighting over parking and food. There was no parking place; most drivers just parked on the shoulder. Finding parking at the end of every day is another task. Truck stops always seem full between six and seven pm. I've gotten myself in a few tight situations where, had it not been for Tammy, I would have never gotten out.

You need a lot of room to turn those trucks around. I've seen drivers go down the wrong road and try turning around with not enough room and get themselves stuck in a ditch or worse. The best thing is to drive in reverse until you can turn around.

One day we were waiting in Dallas for a load and got a call saying her youngest daughter had been in an accident. It was wintertime in Michigan, and she had not been driving long enough to handle driving in the snow. Especially since she had been born in California, she wasn't used to snow. We were lucky enough to get a load home as we were both a bit worried. I dropped Tammy off at home and decided to try and work locally. I hated my job but was lucky enough to pick up a dedicated route to Sheboygan, WI, and back. I stayed with the route for over three years.

One winter, it was so cold with the wind chills twenty to thirty-five below zero for nearly four months straight. As I was driving towards Sheboygan, WI, the glad hand which supplied my trailer brakes with air broke off. Once you no longer have air to your brakes, they lock up. As I was doing sixty-five miles per hour, my trailer brakes locked up, and the trailer started bunny hopping. It was hard enough driving with the freeway covered, and now this? Somehow, I was able to get the truck to the shoulder without flipping over. Talk about scared; my heart was beating like a trip hammer. I had to keep this a secret for a while because my wife had been having these bad feelings about losing me in an accident. I didn't want to freak her out, and since I managed to stop the truck without damage, I got no ticket. The guys I was working for needed someone to do the safety.

While Tammy was riding with me, I taught her what I knew about logs and safety. Since she is one intelligent lady, what I wasn't able to teach her she figured out on her own. These two guys hired her to do their logs and safety. The problem was they were cheap and didn't want to do things legally. It was not the way Tammy and I did things because not doing things legally could cause many issues. She had to quit and come back a few times. She saved them from losing their businesses more than once. The last time neither was acting like they were very grateful nor like the same guys, we had met six years earlier. One was just straight-up being an asshole. The other started up a drinking problem which made him an asshole, as well. They had burned their bridges with Tammy, and she said never again will she do anything for them.

I decided to buy a truck and start my own company. It turned out to be more complicated than we thought, especially since the truck we bought had only a single axle. Meaning we couldn't haul a lot of weight. I met up with a guy who was hauling a flatbed and said he had a forty-eight-foot flatbed that would be perfect for my truck. I stopped hauling vans and joined up with this guy, Bates. He and I did some repairs to my truck and the trailer he had. He was right; it was perfect for my truck. We were doing well at first, then during his home time, he injured himself and twisted his back. He wasn't able to drive, which meant I was the only one making money, and instead of paying me, he paid his bills. He ended up owing me over seven grand and decided to give me the trailer I had been hauling. I was happy about the trailer, but even with the trailer, he still owed me money. When he canceled his insurance, I was no longer able to work, so I drove home and parked both the truck and trailer with no job or money.

I wasn't worried about finding a job; they were everywhere. I found a job working for a company out of Southfield, Mich. The only type of trucks he owned were Volvos. I had only driven a Volvo once, so I didn't know much about them. I had always driven Freightliner's or Kenworth. About a year and a half ago, we found out my brother-in-law, Bud had been diagnosed with stage three brain cancer. The news was devastating since. I lost my stepdad in 2017. I was heartbroken to think of the suffering he would have to endure, and losing another brother was the worst. It's life. We don't live forever; we all will be gone one day. Always m*ake sure the people you love know what they mean to you every day because you never know when one day, you're not able to say I love you. It will be something you will never forget, and it will haunt you for the rest of your life.*

CHAPTER 25

What has the world come to? Now gays are kissing on television in front of my grandkids. How *do you explain why two men are kissing to a three and five-year-old? Am I supposed to tell them that's normal?* Hell no, that shit ain't normal kids should not have to see it. The world is so messed up. I wish we would stop fucking with our kids; they're so confused. Am I a boy, or am I a girl? Am I gay or Bi? Just let these kids be kids. If you are gay, find no reason to advertise it on television or to the world. Please keep that in your own home; I understand not wanting to be hated for how you are but. I personally do not want to see gays kissing or strutting their feelings toward other people.

In 2020, people in China were dying from a virus called Corona (aka) Covid- 19. It started in China in 2019, and the US had its first confirmed case on January 20, 2020. Over five hundred million people have been infected worldwide, with 6,337,189 deaths, as of June 16, 2022. The US alone has had 86,163,137 cases reported, with only 1,015,137 deaths. Now I'm no mathematician, but those are not bad odds. I'm not saying those deaths were not tragic and painful for many folks. For our country to completely shut down, no school, no going out to eat, people didn't even go to work, and a lot of people to this day haven't gone back to work shutting everything down was completely ridiculous. I personally spent Christmas day with nine infected people and slept with my wife for three weeks while she was still contagious and never caught it. As I'm writing this book, I still have yet to catch it. Does that make me lucky; I can't say. Our government ultimately made too big of a deal, and I'm sure some people will disagree. I spent four days waiting to be unloaded at a Walmart Distribution Center because I was delivering bicycles, not food or toilet paper. Talk about pissed off. Driving through Massachusett and New York was like driving through a winter wonderland; it was beautiful. It was getting close to Easter, and my sister wanted my wife and me to spend it with her.

After my delivery in Michigan, it just so happened I was picking up a load in Michigan going to North Carolina. This made me have to drive right close to my sister in Kentucky. My wife originally planned on going with me, but her daughter had an important doctor's appointment that she wanted to attend. The load I was carrying didn't have to be delivered for a few days. I dropped the trailer at the yard and grabbed a new one for my next load. I had to pick up a load of mulch weighing over forty-four thousand pounds. As I was trying to slide my tandems, which are the eight tires on the trailer, so the weight is distributed evenly, I couldn't slide them due to the brakes on the trailer needing adjustment. On my way out of Mich. I stopped by the yard so my boss could adjust them. He said he not only adjusted them but slid the tandems for me. I was running late, so he suggested I should get moving.

As I got close to my sister's place, I called her to come to pick me up at an empty parking lot in town. After getting to her place, I looked forward to seeing my brother-in-law.

As I came into the living room, I nearly started to cry. He was not the same guy I saw the Christmas before. He wasn't talking normally, but now he can't even speak. He was completely dependent on my sister and nieces to care for him. He had to be fed through a tube and wear a diaper. It was hard for me to see him like that. I must have started crying half a dozen times. I was having flashbacks of my best friend, Pat. He had been in the same situation, unable to care for himself.

I spent Saturday and most of Easter Sunday with my sister and family. My sister dropped me off at the truck and said, "Goodbye."

I had a seven-hour drive to make my delivery at the Lowe's Distribution Center in North Carolina. I drove until I got tired, and I was already in NC. I decided to stop and take a nap. I had to be there at eight a.m; after my nap, I did my logs and took off driving down a two-way mountain, meaning I had only one lane to drive in, and the other lane was going in the opposite direction. It was just starting to get daylight, and I noticed I had about an hour to get there. Figuring I would make it on time with only forty minutes left of driving. I noticed up ahead there was an S curve requiring me to slow down. As I started to apply pressure to the brakes, nothing was happening, and I wasn't slowing down.

I immediately reached for the emergency Jake brake for the trailer to slow me down. Realizing this is a Volvo, they don't have a Jake brake, which is a brake in most trucks that helps to stop the truck in an emergency. I was going through ideas of what to do. I knew I couldn't downshift. I was already going too fast and started getting scared. First, I thought maybe I could try to take the curve if I used the left lane. But then I can't see if someone is driving toward me. I had to do whatever my choice was quickly, so I made it. I decided to lay the truck on the passenger side. I figured I might get lucky, and the truck would not slide over the edge of the mountain. I also would not hit anyone coming the other way; I could never live with myself killing an innocent person. This is the second time I've had to make a quick decision to save someone else. The first was when I ran down the hill steering my car from the outside and now. I took the wheel, turned to the right, and then a hard left. I could feel the trailer tipping, so I braced myself for the impact. I felt as if I was having a nightmare. I was hoping I would wake up, but I didn't, and the next thing I knew, my seat belt snapped, and I fell onto the passenger door. I could hear the glass breaking and the screeching sound of the metal against the pavement. I was thinking to myself, please stop sliding, but it slid for over one hundred and twenty-five feet. Finally, it stopped. My first thought was, I have to get out of this truck; my left foot seemed stuck. I couldn't get it loose, so I kept pulling on it. Next, I heard someone yelling, "Can anyone hear me?" He thought I was dead. I yelled back and said, "I'm over here." As he came up behind me, he asked, is there something I can do?" I said, "Yes, please help me out." He stated there was no getting me out. I was wrapped up in metal like a hot dog. As I started feeling pain in my back, I asked if he could get me a blanket or something to put under my back. I was holding almost half my torso off the ground. He went and grabbed a coat and stuffed it under me.

Something was lying across my face tickling my nose. When I reached up, my scalp had nearly been torn off. I could literally feel my skull. It was my hair tickling my nose. I thought I was going to die, so I started to shake. The guy said his name was Jerry, and after calling 911, I heard his description of what I looked like, which scared me even more than he asked if there was someone he could call for me. I said, "Yes, my wife." Then I wasn't sure if I would remember the number. Luckily, I did; as soon as he started describing everything to her, I started to cry. As soon as I heard her voice, all I could say was, "I'm hurting really bad, baby." She said, "Don't worry about anything; I'm getting your mom, and we are on the way."

I could hear the sirens of the fire truck and police. I felt better knowing they were there. One of the responders knelt behind me, telling me my arm was severe and bleeding heavily. He would have to put an IV in it, but it would hurt like hell. Boy, was he right; it hurt like hell. Then a fireman said, "We are going to start cutting you out of there." As soon as he started cutting, it felt like someone was trying to break my spine; all I could do was yell out in pain. The guy behind me yelled for him to stop. He reached his arms underneath me and lifted me. I must have passed out because I only remember bits and pieces of being cut out. I do know it took over an hour. I woke up just as they were pulling me out. As they were putting me in the ambulance, I asked the guy behind me, "Please, come with me." He was the only one I had a connection with, and honestly, I felt alone and quite scared as I was lying there being cut out. I didn't think I would live. I kept thinking am I going to die? The guy was asking me questions about my family. If I was married, how many kids and grandkids did, I have? He said they were going to fly me to the Asheville trauma center. As they were about to put me in the helicopter, my friend said, "I won't be able to fly with you." He took my hand and said, "You'll be fine. I will come to the hospital later to check on you."

I never heard his voice again. I've often thought about trying to find out who he was and just thank him. I was alone once more with no familiar voice. My face was covered because of the injury to my head. After the helicopter lifted off, I passed out again. The next thing I remember, I was being rushed in the hospital. Then I was woken up by a doctor showing me x-rays of my arm and saying he would be putting plates and screws on both bones as they snapped in half. Then some other guy was stapling the top of my head like he was laying carpet. I asked him, What color carpet are you laying?" I was asking, and everyone in the room started laughing; I passed out again. Waking up in my room hoping to see my wife, but the nurse said she couldn't come because of Covid. I was really bothered by the reason I needed to see her. Being alone and miles away from home, I just wanted to see a familiar face.

CHAPTER 26

The next four days were hell. On Wednesday, I went through the worst pain I had ever felt in my life talking to Koler on the phone. I was in tears, and I kept hitting the call nurse button, telling them how much I hurt, but it seemed forever before someone came. I was pretty angry no one had come sooner. I didn't feel I was being treated very well and wondered why because I had been very nice to everyone. I heard someone say it was because I didn't have any insurance. I didn't understand how it would affect the nurses caring for me. These people kept coming in, trying to get me to go to some rehab facility. I said, "No way! I'm going home. Do you think I'm going somewhere that won't allow me to see my family? Not me." Friday came, and I was allowed to go home. They didn't want to keep me with no insurance. I wasn't brokenhearted over it, believe me.

I had to wear this thing they called a turtle shell because I had fractured my back in three places, along with my sternum. They didn't want me to injure my back anymore, so I had to wear it and a neck collar because my neck was also fractured. I wasn't looking like I was ready to party. My sister's house was about three to four hours away, and my mom was going to stay there for a short while. The next morning before leaving, I didn't think I would see my brother-in-law Bud again, alive anyway. It was pretty emotional for both of us. We were both in a wheelchair. I wanted him to know how much I loved him and thought of him as my brother.

It took three days to get home because I could only stand riding in the car for about three hours without having to stop. We got home on Sunday; as we pulled into the drive, I noticed a ramp my son-in-law and grandson built for me knowing I was in a wheelchair and couldn't climb the steps. Tammy's oldest daughter came over with the kids. I was very thankful for the ramp; she had gotten me a bunch of stuff I would need for recovery. Tammy's whole family was there for me. My in-laws helped us financially and with anything they could. Just having their support meant the world to me. I had never had anyone who gave a shit before. I mean, people say they would be there for you, but when it comes down to it, there is always an excuse for why they can't. Actions are louder than words.

I couldn't get off the couch without help or use the restroom and talk about embarrassing having someone wipe my ass and getting up in the middle of the night to go, the bathroom waking Tammy up three or four times a night for pain meds. I felt pretty awful depending on others so much. I've never depended on anyone for anything. At times like this, you truly know who cares and who doesn't.

I survived one of the worst accidents my doctors and therapists had ever seen. I've been called a walking miracle. I fractured my back, in three places, my neck, and this was the second time I'd broken my neck and crushed my left big toe. Snapped my right forearm in half with fourteen staples and countless stitches holding my scalp and face together. I fractured my sternum and right shoulder blade, also stitched up my right ear, and fractured my nose, not to mention the cuts on my arms and back from the glass. I'm alive and thankful, unable to work or drive due to a brain injury. But I never give up. I've thought of giving up more than once, but I just keep going for some reason. I had been told by a few people I should write a book. I thought, *who's got the time?* With running a business, making sure I made enough money to pay the bills and survive. I never thought I would be able to. This accident has made it possible, so maybe it was meant to be. I have nothing but time now.

My first few months of coming home were very hard. I was constantly tired after starting my physical therapy. There wasn't much I was able to do. I was so weak; I was tired just walking from the car. But I pushed myself as hard as I could. At times, I was depressed, so I went into the bedroom and silently cried. Trying not to let Tammy know I was crying. I'm not sure as to why I hid it. I think it was because I felt less than a man. I was the one who made the money. I was the provider, and now I'm not going to be able to do that. I couldn't even eat or write my name with my right arm. I could barely move my fingers. *How would I ever be able to provide?* I was also having problems remembering little things. I once forgot my granddaughter's name. I also found out the hospital in NC did not put plates and screws on both bones. In my forearm, they only did the little bone and put a rod on the big one. It made no fucking sense, especially since the rod was too long. It was almost coming through my elbow. My doc had to take it out. Here I was with still a broken bone in my arm.

By the end of 2020, Covid was getting so bad thousands of people were testing positive every day. Masks were required everywhere. They were checking your temperature for all doctor and therapist appointments. In one place, we got our temperatures taken twice in one building.

2021 was the first full year of the pandemic. People were spending holidays and birthdays separately; they even had funerals on zoom; you couldn't even say a proper goodbye to your loved ones. May of 2020, a white police officer killed a Black man by the name of George Floyd, sparking violence like we haven't seen since Martin Luther King, Jr. This time, there were just as many white people causing the violence as the Blacks, maybe even more. With a group of radicals who called themselves Black Lives Matter. The weird part is a lot of the Blacks did not support them. I saw a video of a Black lady in tears yelling Black lives don't matter because more Blacks are killing Blacks than the whites killing blacks.

She was not the only one who felt that way. I mean, this George Floyd situation went berserk. People were burning businesses all over the country, attacking each other like animals. I have always hoped people would come to realize we are all Americans. We need to stick together; the police officer went to prison as he should have, but to give Mr. Floyd's family an American flag as if he were a veteran. No fuckin way! He should never have lost his life. I agree, but to bury him in a golden casket, treated as if he fought and died for our country, I will never agree it should never have happened; he was a fucking criminal, for Christ's sake.

Our veterans have never been treated that well. We left over fifteen hundred men in Vietnam who have never come home. They are coming home fucked up physically and mentally, and what kind of treatment do they get? Our government believes we, the citizens, should care for them. At the same time, congress gives themselves huge houses. Pay raises and live like kings with bodyguards. Once I was old enough to see the absolute truth about our government, I will never respect any of them for as long as I live.

While everyone else was spending Christmas 2020 separately from their families, our son-in-law decided he wanted his parents to join us from California. Most of us did not think it was a good idea, but we were reassured they would be getting tested before coming and wearing masks. Well, neither happened. I asked the dad on Christmas day did the airport require to see their negative results before boarding the plane. Nope, they also did not even get tested. Not only did they not get tested like we were told, but they also gave nine people Covid, including; my in-laws, my grandkids, and even my wife. I was the only one in the house who never caught it.

CHAPTER 27

With my wife having COPD, I was not very happy; she could have died. Since she is tough as nails, she kicked Covid's ass. It did delay my arm surgery, putting the plates and screws on the prominent bone—that which was supposed to be done in NC.

2020 ended on another lousy note. Donald Trump, the current President, was going against some old geezer who was ready for an old folks home. His name was Joe Biden, the Vice President when Obama was in office. Personally, I don't like Trump; he is an arrogant asshole who has a God complex but was he the better man for the job? Absolutely. He had his downfalls, but then everyone does. Not only was he intelligent, but he also had a pair.

North Korea started acting up, whose President looked like a fat twelve-year-old. They were trying to scare us with their weapons. Ole Trump said, "I fucking dare ya! Try it, and we will bring the fire down on your ass like you have never seen." I liked that little fat boy who decided not to try it.

2021 was a challenging year for me trying to get my strength back and get as much use out of my right arm as possible. Also, my brain trauma was causing me to feel tired all the time. Plus, losing my balance and nearly falling wasn't much fun either.

It also made me reflect on my life which is why I'm writing this book. I've come to realize no one is perfect.

Our family is all we have; sometimes, our friends can be just as important. I've lost a lot of people in my life who I will never forget, and I've also learned many lessons. *Your children are the most important people in your life; not only are they our blood, but they are also our future, so we may live on through their eyes if* we don't show our children the love and respect they deserve. How can they ever love their own children?

We as a country need to see this because when it comes down to it, we are all we have. Without each other, what kind of future can we have? I believe we need to take our country back from the ones who have taken it from us. I don't need to draw a picture for people to understand what I'm saying. As a child, I was raped and beaten by my own father. I had to learn how to come to terms with my abuse. I didn't let it control my life. I fought to be a better man and a better father.

I didn't do so well at being a good husband the first time. It is something I can never forgive myself for. I promised myself I would never marry again until I was positive I could be a better husband. We have had our difficulties, but we fought through them together. I now feel I have been that husband. Of course, our marriage will never be perfect, but then again, no marriage is. It's what you do as a couple. Do you fight through it together, or do you just give up? The choice is yours, but I say never give up. If you truly love each other, there is nothing you can't do.

I've had to fight to survive my whole life. First, I nearly died even before birth; then, I survived being abused in every way possible, sexually, physically, and mentally. I've watched men and women being beaten bloody before my eyes. People are being shot and stabbed and unable to do anything about it. I have lost more people than I can count, one being my best friend. The people from my club, who I thought of as family, never being able to say goodbye, which not only broke my heart but made me feel so alone. Because I never truly felt loved by my own flesh and blood to me, those people were the only ones who did love me. My grandparents even chose my sister over me. To live a life without being loved is the worst feeling in the world which is why I tried taking my own life.

I was meant to live for some reason. I'm still trying to figure it out. I hope it's to make people see what they are doing to themselves. Remember always to let the people you love know how much you love them every day, especially your children; please don't let them suffer the way I did. If you're hurting them, get the help you need. They never forget the pain you're causing, and it will haunt them for the rest of their lives. They need your protection just as I needed my father's. Always remember the people in this country who have lived and died for it. They will always remain our brothers and sisters. JUST Like ME!

ACKNOWLEDGMENTS

I would like to thank some of the people who have encouraged me and have been by my side when I needed it the most. First and foremost my wife Tammy who has stood beside me through it all helped me when I could barely walk and woke up many nights to care for me. To my therapist Jill who kept me going. Especially Dr. Rama who took every phonecall and watched out for me from day one of my accident and last but not least my editor and friend Rebecca